This is a coll... ...ul family run ... ...c interest, offerin... ...nd Ireland. They a... ...s. With a warm w... house & a comf... ...res of this undiscove...ed .... iviany have self catering cottages or can be rented by the week.

The style of accommodation ranges from cosy cottages to grand stately homes. Often the range of facilities & degree of luxury is reflected in the price, but all of them can be highly recommended. They are firstly chosen for their friendliness. Some offer outstanding food, others have a memorable ambiance, or are of exceptional beauty. All are special. You will find indices of houses where languages are spoken, houses that welcome children, & houses that are suitable for the less mobile.

You will also find in each county recommendations from guests who have used the Friendly Homes. The listing includes pubs & inns, special craft shops, thatched houses & cottages, other places to stay, & places worth visiting, generally well away from tour buses. The historic houses that one can visit by day are enormously charming & interesting. Most visitors will see the addictive attraction of sweet disorder (decorators call it shabby chic) that some display. However those who have not previously been exposed to a certain disregard of worldly values may be shocked!

We hope that you enjoy your stay in the Friendly Homes & would welcome any recommendations, comments, praise or complaints to John Colclough, Tourism Resources Ltd PO Box 2281 Dublin 4

For special offers, lots of self catering properties, & more information visit our web pages at www.tourismresources.ie

Central bookings via fax at +353 1 668 6578 or e-mail cht@indigo.ie

> Remember to let your hosts know your arrival time
>
> Be sure to book dinner in advance
>
> Prices are per person sharing based on double occupancy
>
> If you have to cancel there may be a cancellation charge - check when booking

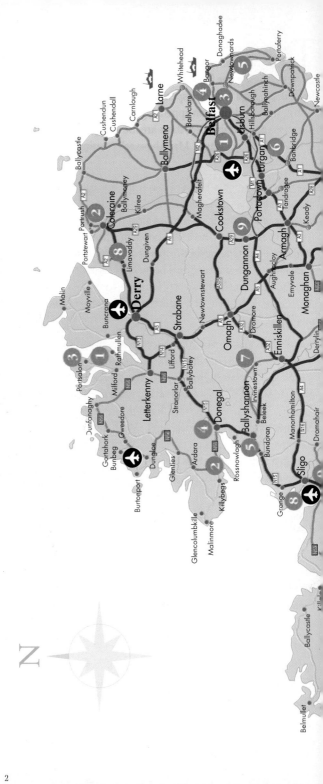

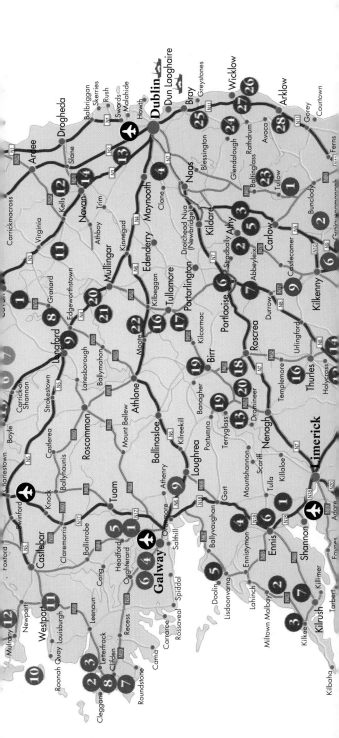

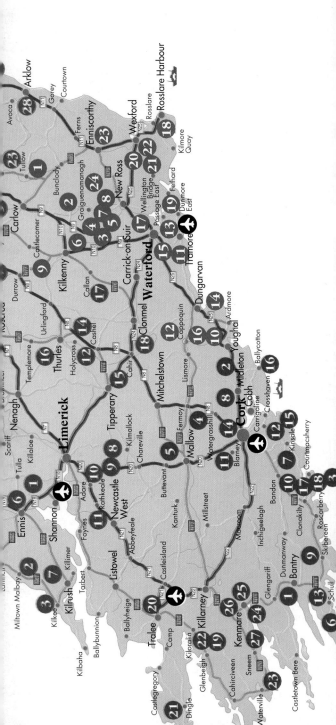

4

Fr: Francais   Sw: Sweedish   Gr: Deutsch   Ch: Chinese
Ir: Irish   Sp: Espanol   Du: Dutch   It: Italiano

INDEX

A1 **ABERDEEN LODGE**, Pat Halpin
53/55 PARK AVE, BALLSBRIDGE, DUBLIN 4
Tel (01) 2838155 **Fax** (01) 2837877 <aberdeen@iol.ie>

MERRION HALL,
54-56 MERRION ROAD, DUBLIN 4
Tel (01) 6681426 **Fax** (01) 6684280
US 1 800 223 6510 <merrionhall@iol.ie>

B & B £35.00 - £65.00 €44-82 **DINNER** - room service menu
SINGLE SUPPLEMENT £20.00 €25

Excellent sister guesthouses 4* luxury, RAC Highly acclaimed award. AA 5 diamond. Elegant combination of earl Edwardian grace & every modern comfort, including suites with jacuzzi executive facilities. Private gardens, parking. Gym & golf nearby. Superb location, convenient to DART, city centre & airport. Open all year. Full licence. Children welcome. Credit car 15 en suite rooms & 4 suites at Aberde Lodge 19 en suite rooms, 3 suites & 3 executive rooms at Merrion Hall.

A2 **ASHBROOK HOUSE**, Eve Mitchell
RIVER ROAD, ASHTOWN, CASTLEKNOCK, DUBLIN 15
Tel & **Fax** (01) 8385660

B & B £25.00 - £30.00 €32-38 **SINGLE SUPPLEMENT** £10.00 €12

A beautiful old Georgian country house on 10 acres, beside the Phoenix Park. 10 mins. city centre & 15 mins. airport. Close to good pubs. Ideal location for visiting Dublin. Golfing, fishing, racing nearby. Secure car parking, tennis court & walled gardens. Open 2/01 - 20/12. Credit cards. 4 en-suite rooms with direct dial telephone.

A3 **BELCAMP HUTCHINSON**, Karl Waldburg - Doreen Gleeson
CARR'S LANE, MALAHIDE RD, BALGRIFFIN, DUBLIN 17
Tel (01) 846 0843 **Fax** (01)848 5703

B & B £44.00 €56 Single supplement £44.00

A Classical Georgian house (1786) restored to the highest standard. Set in 4 acres of landscaped gardens. Close to airport, Dublin city, beaches & golf courses nearby. Ask for brochure. Open 01/01-22/12. Credit cards. 6 en-suite rooms.

4 CUMBERLAND LODGE, David & Mariea Jameson
4 YORK ROAD, DUN LAOGHAIRE,
Tel (01) 280 9665 **Fax** (01)2843227 <cumberlandlodge@eircom.net>

B & B £30.00 €35   **SINGLE SUPPLEMENT** £5.00

Beautifully restored Georgian home. Decorated in rich colours & fabrics, with antiques & open fires, where a warm welcome awaits you. Secure parking. Ferry 4 min. DART 5 min. ideal for touring city centre, Wicklow & S. E. AA 4 diamond Open all year Credit cards 4 en suite rooms with t.v & dd tel.

5 DRUID LODGE, Ken & Cynthia McClenaghan
KILLINEY HILL RD, KILLINEY, CO DUBLIN
Tel (01) 285 1632 **Fax** (01) 284 8504

B & B from £28.00 €35 **SINGLE SUPPLEMENT** £10.00 €12

Charming early Victorian manor overlooking Killiney Bay on 1 acre of private grounds. A peaceful atmosphere enhanced by a fine reputation for hospitality. 10 min. from Killiney Hill's spectacular views, Killiney Strand, DART station & Dalkey's good restaurants & pubs. City centre 25 mins. by DART Dunlaoghaire ferry 2 miles. Open all year. Credit cards. 4 en suite rooms.

6 THE HIBERNIAN HOTEL, Siobhan Maher, Manager
EASTMORELAND PLACE, BALLSBRIDGE, DUBLIN 4.
Tel (01)668 7666 Fax(01)660 2655 <info@hibernianhotel.com>

B from £75 €94 (plus breakfast) **DINNER** £35.00 €44
SINGLE SUPPLEMENT from £45.00 €25

A perfect alternative to the larger city hotels. The Hibernian is one of the friendliest homes in Dublin. A member of Small Luxury Hotels of the World. Open 28/12 - 23/12. Dinner 6.30pm - 10.00pm, book by 6pm. Full licence. Credit cards. 40 en-suite rooms.

A7 NUMBER 31, Noel & Deidre Comer,
31 LEESON CLOSE, DUBLIN 2.
Tel (01) 6765011 **Fax** (01) 6762929 <number31@iol.ie>

B & B £42.50-65.00 €55-85 **SINGLE SUPPLEMENT** £11.00 €14

Award winning guesthouse in the heart of Georgian Dublin. Former home of leading architect Sam Stephenson. An oasis of tranquillity & greenery just off St Stephen's Green. Vast breakfasts & a warm welcome. Secure car parking. Recommended by Bridgestone, Good Hotel Guide & Egon Ronay. Open 28/12 - 21/12. Credit cards. Children over 10 welcome. 18 en suite rooms.

A8 RAGLAN LODGE, Helen Moran
10 RAGLAN RD., BALLSBRIDGE, DUBLIN 4
Tel (01) 6606697 **Fax** (01) 6606781

B&B £40.00-£55.00 **SINGLE SUPPLEMENT** £10.00

Impressive Victorian townhouse on an exclusive, quiet leafy street in historic preservation area, 15 minute walk from Stephen's Green, & beside the US Embassy & Herbert Park. Open 16/01-18/12 Credit cards. 7 ensuite rooms.

A9 SIMMONSTOWN HOUSE, James & Finola Curry
2 SYDENHAM ROAD, BALLSBRIDGE DUBLIN 4
Tel (01) 6607260 **Fax** (01) 6607341 < simmons@indigo.ie >

B&B £40-50.00, **SINGLE SUPPLEMENT** £10.00

A favoured "home from home" for discerning guests, this elegant Victorian townhouse is 10 minutes from the city centre by Bus or DART & a gentle stroll from the restaurants of Ballsbridge & the Four Seasons Hotel. Off street parking available. Open mid Jan - Mid Dec Credit Cards 4 en suite rooms

10 **TRINITY LODGE**, Peter Murphy
2 SOUTH FREDERICK STREET, DUBLIN 2.
Tel (01) 679 5044 **Fax** (01) 679 5223 <trinitylodge@eircom.net>

B & B from £47.50 €60 **SINGLE SUPPLEMENT** £40.00 €50

In the heart of Dublin, it offers superb accommodation in a traditional Georgian townhouse. All of Dublin's business, shopping, historic centres, Trinity College & Grafton Street on the door step. Each room, from the singles to the 650 square suites has air conditioning, DD phone, personal safe, radio alarm clock, satellite TV, trouser press & tea/coffee making facilities. Open 1/01 - 31/12. Credit cards. Children welcome. 13 en-suite rooms.

11 **WILLOWBROOK**, Joseph & Mary Mooney
4 STRANDVILLE AVE. EAST, CLONTARF, DUBLIN 3.
Tel (01) 8333115 <willowbrook@ireland.com>

B & B £25.00 €32 **SINGLE SUPPLEMENT** £15.00 €19

A new, gracious detached home on a quiet street in Old Clontarf. 10 mins. city centre, Dublin Port, Point Theatre. Airport 20 mins. Fresh flowers, fine furniture & paintings & a warm friendly Irish welcome make your visit memorable. Golf, sailing & bird sanctuary nearby. Great value for business, touring & sporting occasions. Secure parking. Minimum stay 2 nights Open 30/12 - 20/12. 3 en suite rooms.

READERS ALSO RECOMMEND

Hollybrook Park House, 10 Hollybrook Park, Clontarf, Dublin 3 Frank & Jean Shouldice, (01) 8339656. B&B £22.50-£24.00, €28. Single supplement £5.00 Much altered characterful 18th C. house on quiet road with lovely garden. Open 1/03-31/10 3 rooms, 2 en suite.

Newtown House, St Margaret's, Co. Dublin (01) 8341081, Sheila Wilson-Wright B&B from £40.00 €54 single supplement £5.00 €6. Elegant 18th Century house surrounded by 18 hole open golf course with driving range, 10 minutes from the airport. Open 6/01-16/12 Unsuitable for children, no pets. 2 twin rooms, 2 bathrooms.

South Lodge, Strand Road, Portmarnock. (01) 8461356 Pat & Colin Burton B&B about €23.00 1870s lodge, 2 minutes from the beach & 15 minutes from the airport.

PUBS

O'Neills Victorian Pub & Townhouse, Gerry O'Neill 36-37 Pearce Street, Dublin 2 Tel (01) 6714074 Fax (01) 8325218 <oneilpub@iol.ie > B&B £20.00-£45.00 €25 - 60. Refurbished in 1998, The O'Neill family have dispensed their famous hospitality here, between Trinity College & The River Liffey, for over 100 years. Meals served all day. Credit cards. 6 double rooms, 2 family rooms, all en suite.

PUBS *continued*

Johnny Foxes, Glencullen, (01) 2955647 famous hostelry in the Dublin Mountains with food & entertainment.

Café en Seine 40 Dawson St, Dublin 2 (01) 6774369 The fashionable place to be seen, & an enjoyable place to people watch

RESTAURANTS

There are hundreds of restaurants in Dublin, from burger bars to haute cuisine, but there are some very special places in the countryside around the city.
The Old Schoolhouse in Swords is excellent, as is **Red Bank Restaurant & Guesthouse**, Terry & Margaret McCoy, 6-7 Church St Skerries Co Dublin
Tel (01) 8491005 Fax (01) 8491598 <redbank@eircom.net>
Delightful seaside village restaurant with famous chef proprietor. Seafood a speciality
Average dinner £26.00 B&B £25-£35 12 en suite rooms.

HERITAGE ATTRACTIONS

Trinity College, **St Patrick's Cathedral** & **Dublin Castle** are "must sees" for everyone. Memorable sites are often the less visited. Two favourites are:

Drimnagh Castle, Long Mile Road, Dublin 12, (01) 4502530
Open Sat & Sun 12.00-17.00

Fernhill Gardens, Sandyford, Co Dublin (01) 2956000 40 acres of parkland, woodland, rockery & water garden situated 7 miles south of the city. Open March to September Tues-Sat & Bank Holidays 11.00-5.00. Sundays 2.00-5.00 Admission £3.00 OAPs/Students £2.00

OUNTY CAVAN

SUNNYSIDE HOUSE Dieter & Bridget Koston
UGH GOWNA, CO CAVAN **Tel/Fax** (043) 83285

& B £25.00 €32 **DINNER** £20.00 €19

A turn of the century doctor's residence, modernised but still exuding the easy charm of the era. The relaxing gardens provide fresh fruit, herbs, honey & vegetables for seasonal cuisine. Ample information on places of interest, open gardens & houses, is readily available in rooms. Open all year. Dinner 7.30pm, book by 2pm.. 4 bedrooms.

READERS ALSO RECOMMEND in Co. Cavan

ockwood House, James & Susan McCauley Cloverhill Tel (047) 55351 Fax (047) 373 <jbmac@eircom.net> B&B £20.00, €25. Pretty reconstructed Victorian house. en all year except Christmas. Children welcome. Dogs allowed. 4 en suite rooms.

iverside House, Cootehill Joe & Una Smith, (049)5552150 &B around £20.00 4 en suite rooms

isnamandra, Crossdoney, Co Cavan (049) 4337196 B&B about £18.00, €23. Friendly rmhouse. Open May - Oct. 4 rooms, 3 en suite.

UBS

he Keepers Arms, Bawnboy (049) 9523318 peaceful & pretty pub with commodation B&B about £20.00, €25

erragarra Inn, Butlersbridge (049) 4331003 Tons of character & good food in an area at is well worth exploring

he Welcome Inn, Swalinbar, (049) 9521230 B&B from £16.00 €20

ERITAGE ATTRACTIONS

Maudabawn Cultural Centre, Cootehill (049) 5559504 a short walk through 000 years of Irish history.

COUNTY KILDARE

2 COURSETOWN HOUSE, Iris & James Fox
TRADBALLY ROAD, ATHY, CO.KILDARE
el (0507) 31101 **Fax** (0507) 32740

& B 30.00 €33 **SINGLE SUPPLEMENT** $5.00 €6

Delightful & very comfortable 200 year old farmhouse with great breakfasts Rural setting, but only 2 minutes from Athy. RAC "sparkling diamond" award Open 01/01-23/12. Credit cards. 4 ensuite rooms

B3 **GRIESEMOUNT**, Robert & Carolyn Ashe
BALLITORE, CO. KILDARE.
Tel (0507) 23158 **Fax** (0503) 40687 <griesmount@eircom.net>

B & B £25.00 - £35.00 €25-38 **SINGLE SUPPLEMENT** £5.00 €6
DINNER £20.00

A small & very pretty Georgian house set outside the historic Quaker village of Ballitore. Comfortable rooms & friendly, relaxed atmosphere. Ideal golfing centre - Rathsallagh Golf Course 4 miles, Carlow Championship Golf Course 10 miles. The Curragh & Punchestown nearby. Dublin, Kilkenny & Glendalough under 1 hour. Good local restaurants. Stay 2 nights - 3rd night free! Open 15/01 - 30/11. Dogs allowed outside. 3 ensuite rooms.

B4 **SPRINGFIELD**, Libby Sheehy
CELBRIDGE, CO KILDARE. **Tel** (01) 6273248 **Fax** (01) 6273123

B & B £35.00 -£75.00 €44 - €90 **DINNER** from £30.00 €38

Splendidly comfortable & discrete accommodation in a haven of Georgian tranquillity only 12 miles from Dublin. Refurbished by its present owner to a very high standard. Minutes from one of Ireland's finest golf course, the K Club. Dinner for private parties can be arranged. Open all year. Credit cards. 6 en-suite rooms.

B5 **TONLEGEE HOUSE**, Mark & Marjorie Molloy
ATHY, CO. KILDARE.
Tel & Fax (0507) 31473 <tonlegeehouse@eircom.net>

B & B £37.50 - 45.00 €48 **DINNER** £25.00 €32
SINGLE SUPPLEMENT £12.50 €16

Restored by the Molloys as a country house & restaurant of warmth & character. 5 min. Athy, hr Dublin, An ideal place to stay for either an activity filled or leisurely break. Some rooms with 4 poster beds RAC Merit award for Restaurant & Hospitality. Egon Ronay & Bridgestone recommended Dinner 7-9pm. Open all year except Christmas. Full licence. Credit cards. 9 en suite rooms.

READERS ALSO RECOMMEND in Co. Kildare

rberstown Castle, Straffan The nearest castle to Dublin that offers accommodation
) 6288157 B&B from £60.00+ €76

artinstown House, The Curragh (045) 441269 Grand & elegant gothic lodge,
utedly built as a ducal love nest B&B around £50.00 €63

JBS

ken Thomas, The Square, Kildare (045) 521695 Bar food & a well crafted traditional
erior in the heart of this historic town.

oone High Cross Inn, John Clynch, Bolton Hill, Moone (0507) 24112 B&B: £25.00+
30 18th C. award winning country inn with food all day & story telling & singing on
turday nights 5 en suite rooms.

ne Ballymore Inn, Ballymore Eustace (045) 864585 Sophisticated country pub,
cellent food & an attractive village, 45 minutes from Dublin. A small detour off the
aten track & well worth it.

ne Johnstown Inn, Johnstown, Naas, (045)897547 Quiet historic village, 40 minutes
m Dublin. A traditional pub with Irish music.

rney's Kilcullen, (045) 481804/481260 Excellent food in the restaurant & a
spitable bar to relax in just by the Liffey Bridge.

rey's Moyvalley, (0405) 51185 Old fashioned bar, where the road, railway & canal
et in the middle of nowhere, between Enfield & Moyvalley. Great snacks.

ERITAGE ATTRACTIONS

rchill Arcadian Gardens Kilcock, Tel (01)628 7354 Fax (01)628 4580 Ornamental garden
18th century origin Walk through a landscape of follies & exotic animal breeds
lmission: £3.50

COUNTY LAOIS

6 IVYLEIGH, Dinah & Jerry Campion
ANK PLACE, PORTLAOISE
l (0502) 22081 **Fax** (0502) 63343 <ivyleigh@gofree.indigo.ie>

&B £35.00 €45 **SINGLE SUPPLEMENT** £5.00 €6

5 Diamond. RAC "Little Gem"
award. Recently refurbished,
luxurious, listed Georgian
townhouse. Excellent service &
superb breakfasts, combined with
traditional Irish warmth &
friendliness. Close to town centre
& railway station, Slieve Bloom
Mountains, Historic houses &
gardens, riding, golf & fishing
locally. Open 07/01-20/12 5
ensuite rooms.

READERS ALSO RECOMMEND in Co. Laois

hez Nous, Kilminchy, Dublin Road, Portlaoise (0502) 21251.
udrey and Tony Canavan.
ylish contemporary house with famous breakfasts. B&B £25.00 €30.

B7 **PRESTON HOUSE**, Allison & Michael Dowling
MAIN STREET, ABBEYLEIX, CO LAOIS.
Tel & **Fax** (0502) 31432

B & B £25.00 €32
DINNER A LA CARTE
SINGLE SUPPLEMENT £5.00 €6

Noble stone ivy clad building, furnished with antiques. Spacious bedrooms, private parking. 60 miles Dublin. Heywood Gardens & Slieve Bloom mountains close by. Open 01/03 - 31/01 except Christmas. Dinner 6-9pm, book by 6pm. Wine licence. Credit cards. 4 en suite rooms.

READERS ALSO RECOMMEND in Co. Laois

Roundwood House, Mountrath (0502) 32120 Charming Georgian manor with good food B&B £44.00 €50 Dinner 24.00 €30 Open Jan - Dec 10 en suite rooms.

Tullamoy House, Stradbally, Pat & Caroline Farrell (0507) 27111 B&B £22.00 €28 Sing supplement ££5.00, Dinner £15.00. Pleasant 19th century farmhouse beside an ancient castle, with large drawing room & dining room for relaxing & enjoying a fresh farm breakfasts Open 01/01-20/12 4 en suite rooms.

PUBS

The Fisherman's Inn, Fisherstown, Ballybrittas, Co Laois (0502) 26488 Cosy ramblin thatched bar, a remote cross roads on the 18th C. main road to the West. Just off the Cork Dublin road. Wild ceilis some evenings. Other times sit outside & listen to hens cackling.

Morrissey's Bar, Abbeyleix, Co Laois (0502) 31233 Famed throughout the land - the finest original Victorian interior in Ireland.

Foxrock Inn, Sean & Marian Hyland, Clough, Ballacolla (0502) 38637 <foxrockinn@eircom.net> B&B £20.00 €25 Rural pub with accommodation & music on Fri. & Sat nights. 6 en suite rooms.

Vicarstown Inn, Vicarstown (0502) 25189 pub with accommodation. B&B under £20.00 €25

Village Inn, Coolrain (0502) 35126 Thatched pub with food by locals for locals, but strangers are welcomed, even by the mountainy men.

COUNTY LONGFORD

B8 **TOBERPHELIM HOUSE**, Dan & Mary Smyth
GRANARD, CO. LONGFORD.
Tel & **Fax** (043) 86568 <tober@eircom.net>

B & B £20.00 - £25.00 €25 - 32 **DINNER** £17.00 €22
SINGLE SUPPLEMENT £10.00 €12

Georgian farmhouse on 200 acre cattle & sheep farm. Warm family hospitality. Traditional cooking served on large mahogany dining table. Fresh spring water. 2km from Granard signposted. Ideal Northern stopover. AAQQQ approved. Open May-Oct. or by arrangement. Wine licence. Dinner 7.30pm, book previous night. Credit cards. Dogs allowed outside. 3 rooms, 2 en-suite

B

9 VIEWMOUNT HOUSE, James & Beryl Kearney
DUBLIN ROAD, LONGFORD **Tel** (043) 41919

B&B £25.00-£35.00 €32- 44 **SINGLE SUPPLEMENT** £5.00 €6

Historic house, dating from 1750, & set in 4 acres of beautiful gardens overlooking golf course. with a small gourmet restaurant It has been recently refurbished, retaining the original character & style of the house. An easy drive from Dublin, & a great base to explore the Lakelands & River Shannon. Tennis & bicycles available Open all year Credit cards Children welcome.. 5 en suite rooms.

HERITAGE ATTRACTIONS

Carrigglas Manor , Longford (043) 45165 Gothic revival manor inhabited by the descendants of the original owner, the inspiration for Mr. Darcy in Pride & Prejudice.

PUBS

Lyon's Bar, Ardagh (043) 75004 Pub with accommodation B&B under £20.00 €25

The River Inn, Ballymahon (0902) 32230 Pub with accommodation.
B&B about £15.00 €19

COUNTY LOUTH

10 COOLEY LODGE Geraldine & Freeman Lynn
MOUNTBAGNAL, Nr. CARLINGFORD, RIVERSTOWN
Tel (042) 76201

B&B £35.00-£40.00 **SINGLE SUPPLEMENT** £10.00

Unique stone building discretely converted into stylish home. Fine ensuite guest rooms, some with idyllic mountain views, 25m. indoor pool. Tennis court. Convenient to beaches & mountain walking. Superb restaurants in nearby Carlingford. Open 01/05-31/10 5 ensuite rooms. Self catering cottage available.

READERS ALSO RECOMMEND in Co. Louth

Balrobin House, Kilkerley, Dundalk (042) 9377701 B&B £35.00-40.00

Ghan House, Carlingford (042) 9373682 B&B from £35.00 €45. 18th C. house between sea & mountain. 12 en-suite rooms.

Jordans, Carlingford (042) 9373223 A restaurant with rooms run by charismatic chef Harry Jordan in this historic town B&B £35.00 €44+.

Red House, Ardee (041) 6853523 Pleasant 18th C. home with indoor pool & tennis court B&B around £40.00 €50.

Lis Narann House, Annagassan, Dunleer. (042) 9372254. B&B from £30.00 €39. Historic seaside home.

COUNTY MEATH

B11 LOUGHCREW HOUSE, Charles & Emily Naper
OLDCASTLE, CO. MEATH.
Tel (049) 8541356 **Fax** (049) 8541722 < cnaper@eircom.net >

B & B £35.00 €44 **DINNER** £20.00 €25
SINGLE SUPPLEMENT £10.00 €13

Delightful converted conservatory magnificent parkland landscape, beside Loughcrew Historic Garden & prehistoric Loughcrew Cairns. Fine furniture & paintings, log fires & fresh flowers create a warm, friendly atmosphere. Tennis, bicycles, splendid trees, woodland walks, lake; Open 10/01 - 20/12. Dinner 8.00 pm, book previous day Credit cards. 3 en suite rooms.

B12 MOUNTAINSTOWN, John & Diana Pollock
CASTLETOWN, NAVAN, CO. MEATH.
Tel (046) 54154/54195 **Fax** (046)54154

B & B £25.00 - £55.00 €32-70 **DINNER** £15.00 to £20.00 €19-25
SINGLE SUPPLEMENT £5.00-20.00 €6-25

Beautifully restored late 17th c. house. Bright & sunny main room. Purchased by the Pollocks in 1796 from Samuel Gibbons, it is a beautiful sporting estate, stock farm, 18th c. courtyard with spring wells, carriage wash, wonderful trees, parkland, donkeys, free roaming poultry & peacocks. Open 3/01 - 22/12. Discount for children. Small dogs allowed. Dinner 8.00pm book 24 hrs in

advance. 3 superb en suite bedrooms (1 four poster) 3 other rooms in Georgian wing, also available for self-catering

B13 THE OLD WORKHOUSE, Niamh & Dermod Colgan
DUNSHAUGHLIN, CO MEATH.
Tel/Fax (01) 8259251 <comfort@a-vip.com>

B & B £30.00 - £45.00 €38-51
SINGLE SUPPLEMENT £10.00 - £15.00 €12-19
DINNER £25.00 -£30 €32 (Min 6 persons, only available Oct. - May)

Listed 1841 historic building, beautifully restored. Comfortable & relaxed atmosphere. Local garden & historic tours arranged. Convenient for shopping, racing, golfing & hunting. On Navan Road (N3), 20 minutes Dublin Airport & city & 45 minutes Dun Laoghire ferry. Bridgestone Award. AAQQQQ selected. RAC highly acclaimed. Excellent food. Open 1/01 to 20/12. Dinner 7.30 pm, book previous day. Credit cards. 5 en suite rooms.

B14 SWYNNERTON LODGE, Trevor FitzHerbert
BLACK CASTLE, NAVAN, CO. MEATH
Tel/Fax (046)21371

B & B - £25.00 €25 - 32 **DINNER** £16.00 €19
SINGLE SUPPLEMENT £7.00 €8

Fishing lodge overlooking the River Boyne on private 400 acre estate. Entrance 1km from Navan on main road to Slane(N51). Extensive fishing rights. Tennis court & barbecue room. Hunting, riding & golf arranged. Central for touring historic sites. Dublin airport 40km. Dinner 8pm, book previous day. Open 1/03-01/10, off season by arrangement. Credit cards. 5 rooms, 4 en suite.

READERS ALSO RECOMMEND in Co. Meath

Annesbrook, Duleek, Kate Sweetman, 041 9823293 Pretty historic house, B&B around £30.00 €38

Boltown House, Kells, Jean Wilson, Tel (046) 43605 Fax (046) 43036 18th C. farmhouse B&B £32.00 €34. Dinner £24.00 €30 Relaxed & comfortable 18th century house, 1 1/4 hr from Dublin.

O'Connell's Bar, Hill of Skyrne, Tara (046) 25122 a pub with tradition.

RESTAURANTS

Hudson's Bistro, Richard & Tricia Hudson, 30 Railway St, Navan
Tel (046) 29231 Fax (046) 73382 <Richard-Hudson@esatclear.ie>
Informal evenings only bistro with original Thai, Italian, Irish & Cajun menu, serving some of the best food in Meath. Dinner about £25.00

HERITAGE ATTRACTIONS

Butterstream Gardens, Trim (046) 36017 Jim Reynolds' Irish Sissinghurst created since the 1970s. Open April-September. Admission: £3.00

COUNTY MONAGHAN

B15 GLYNCH HOUSE, John & Martha O'Grady
NEWBLISS,
Tel & **Fax** (047) 54045 <mirth@eircom.net>

B&B £23.00 - £25.00 €29-32 **DINNER** £15.00 €19
SINGLE SUPPLEMENT £5.00 €6

The genius of the famous architect Richard Morrison. has given Glynch the happy combination of Georgian spaciousness & style, nestling in the heart of drumlin countryside. Antique furnishings. Riding, golf, hunting, Hilton gardens. Browse through numerous antique stores. On Clones/Newbliss R183 road. 500 yards from Newbliss. Belfast airport 56 miles, Dublin airport 67 miles. Open 01/03-30/09 or by arrangement. Dinner 7.00 pm, book by midday. Credit cards. 5 bedrooms, 3 en-suite.

READERS ALSO RECOMMEND in Co. Monaghan

Castle Leslie, Glaslough, (047) 88109 B&B from £55.00 The home of the eccentric Leslies for the last 300 years - ghosts, grandeur, secret corridors, splendid bedrooms, glorious scenery, total tranquility. €69 14 en suite rooms

Fortsingleton House, Emyvale, (047) 86054 B&B around £30.00 €38

PUBS

McEllos Bar, Inniskeen (042) 9378355 the poet Patrick Kavanagh's local when he wasn't observing pretty girls on Raglan Road. Visit the Kavanagh Centre as well.

COUNTY OFFALY

B16 **RAHAN LODGE**, Carole Mc Demott
KILLINA, TULLAMORE, CO OFFALY
Tel (0506) 55753/55796 **Fax** (0506) 55606 <rahan@eircom.net>

B & B £30.00 €38 **DINNER** £20.00 €25

Built by Henry Petty in 1745, this country house is set in the heart of the midlands in a tranquil setting, where you can enjoy comfort & seclusion with good food & log fires. Direct dial telephone in all rooms. Dinner 7.00pm, book by noon. Open Mar.- Oct. Credit Cards. 5 bedrooms, 2 en suite.

B17 **SHEPHERDS WOOD**, Eileen & Johann MacSweeney-Thieme
SCREGGAN, TULLAMORE, CO. OFFALY.
Tel/Fax (0506) 21499 <jgott@esatclear.ie>

B & B £24.00   €30 **DINNER** £25.00 €32
SINGLE SUPPLEMENT £8.00 €12

1930's country house designed by Michael Scott; on 50 acres of forest & peatland, a private wildlife sanctuary. Historical connections with "Irish Mist" & "Tullamore Dew", legendary liquors distilled until recently at Tullamore. Outdoor swimming pool, sauna, croquet, short tennis, wilderness walks, peacocks & Jacob sheep. Open 01/04-30/09. Dinner not always available - book previous day. 4 en-suite rooms. Self catering chalet available. 2 bed, sleeps 4, from £300.00 p.w. €380

READERS ALSO RECOMMEND in Co. Offaly

Ardmore House, The Walk, Kinnitty, Christina Byrne, (0509) 37009 B&B £20.00 €25 Fine Victorian village house, with comfortable rooms and a friendly atmosphere beside Slieve Bloom Mountains. Open all year. 2 en suite rooms, 3 other rooms.

318 SHINRONE HOUSE, Buddy & Pat Lowe
MAIN STREET, SHINRONE, CO OFFALY
Tel (0505) 47292 **Fax** (0505)47419 <shinrone@iol.ie>

B & B £18.00 - £22.00 €22-27 **SINGLE SUPPLEMENT** £7.00 €9

A historic house restored by its American owners to provide very comfortable accommodation in this charming quiet village, near Roscrea, & the main Dublin - Limerick road. Birr Castle & Gardens, Bog Train, golfing, riding, fishing & pubs are a few of the local attractions. Unsuitable for children. Open 7/1-16/12. 4 en-suite bedrooms.

319 SPINNERS TOWN HOUSE, Joe & Fiona Breen
CASTLE STREET, BIRR, CO OFFALY.
Tel & **Fax** (0509)21673 <spinners@indigo.ie>

B & B £17.50 - £20.00 €22-25 **DINNER** around £15.00 €19
SINGLE SUPPLEMENT £5.00 - £7.50 €6-9

We offer a simple concept - recognising & reflecting the needs of the modern tourist in Ireland. Experiencing different cultures & ways of life is a daily occurrence here. We celebrate the landscape & visual inspiration of the Irish Midlands. A pleasant destination to relax, enjoy local food & sleep in comfort & tranquillity. Open 17/3 - 31/10. Dinner 5pm-10pm, Bistro Credit cards. 9 rooms, en suite.

COUNTY WESTMEATH

320 LOUGH OWEL LODGE, Martin & Aideen Ginnell
CULLION, MULLINGAR, CO. WESTMEATH.
Tel (044) 48714 **Fax** (044) 48771 <aginnell@hotmail.com>

B & B £19.00 - £21.00 €24-26 **DINNER** £14.00 €17
SINGLE SUPPLEMENT £6.00 €7

Interesting country lodge set in mature trees overlooking Lough Owel. Friendly family atmosphere, ideal for either an activity filled or relaxing holiday. AAQQQQ Antique furnishings including bedrooms with four-poster beds. Private tennis court. Experience the peace of rural living golf fishing & equestrian facilities nearby. Centrally situated for touring the many historical sites in the area Open 17/3 - 30/11. Dinner 7 pm - book by noon. Credit cards. Dogs allowed outside. 5 en suite rooms

B21 **MEARESCOURT**, Eithne Pendred
RATHCONRATH, MULLINGAR, CO. WESTMEATH.
Tel (044)55112

B & B £27.50-30.00 €35-38 **DINNER** £18.00 €22
SINGLE SUPPLEMENT £10.00 €13

Beautiful & gracious Georgian mansion. Ancient trees & sweeping parkland. Log fires. Seclusion, elegance & spaciousness combined with 20th century comfort. Central location. Warm welcome & delicious home cooking await you. Dinner 7pm, book by noon. Credit cards. Open 2/01 - 20/12. Wine licence. Dogs allowed outdoors. 4 en-suite rooms.

B22 **TEMPLE SPA**, Declan & Bernadette Fagan
HORSELEAP, MOATE, CO. WESTMEATH.
Tel (0506)35118 **Fax** (0506) 35008 <templespa@spiders.ie>

B & B £40.00 - £50.00 €50-65 **DINNER** £20.00 €25
SINGLE SUPPLEMENT £10.00-£20.00 €13-26

250 year old farmhouse with lovely garden in parkland setting, acclaimed for relaxed ambience & excellent cuisine. AAQQQQ. Bridgestone recommended. Large comfortable rooms, antique furnishings. Optional spa programme includes massage & beauty treatments (seaweed, hydrotherapy, yoga, relaxation classes, sauna & steamroom). Ideal for a relaxing break or interlude on a touring holiday. English language holidays. Open all year except Christmas & New Year. Credit cards. Children welcome. Dinner 7.30 pm, book by 10 am. Wine licence. 2 night min. at w/e 8 en-suite rooms.

READERS ALSO RECOMMEND in Co. Westmeath

Cornaher House, Tyrellspass, (044) 23311, Nowell Treacy, B&B around £20.00 Early 19th C. house on 150 organic acres of parkland. 4 ensuite rooms.

Reynella House, Braclyn, Mullingar, Co Westmeath (044) 61437 elegant 18th C. house with lake offering B&B from around £20.00 €25.

PUBS

Grogan's, Glasson, (0902) 85158 pub in Goldsmith's Village of Roses

HERITAGE ATTRACTIONS

Tullynally Castle, Castlepollard Tel (044)61159 Fax (044)61856 <tpakenham@eircom.net> Reference Thomas & Valerie Pakenham, Large rambling gothic revival castle, Home of Earls of Longford since the 1600s. 30 acres of romantic Regency gardens with newly constructed Chinese & Tibetan gardens. Gardens open May - Aug. 2.00-6.00 Castle June 15-July 30 £4.50 castle & gardens, £3.00 gardens only.

COUNTY WICKLOW

B23 **BARRADERRY HOUSE**, Clive & Olive Hobson
KILTEGAN, **Tel** & **Fax** (0508) 73209

B&B £22.50-£25.00 €28-31 **SINGLE SUPPLEMENT** £2.50 €3

Beautiful & relaxing Georgian house at the foot of the Wicklow Mountains. 6 excellent golf courses & 3 race courses within easy reach. Ideal base for touring the South East. Dublin just over 1 hour. AA QQQQ. Open 15.1-15.12 Children welcome. 4 en suite rooms.

B24 **DERRYBAWN HOUSE**, Donald & Lucy Vambeck
GLENDALOUGH, CO. WICKLOW.
Tel (0404) 45134 **Fax** (0404) 45109

B & B £27.50 - £32.50 €34 - 41 **DINNER** £18.50 €23
SINGLE SUPPLEMENT £12.50 €16

Georgian house on 90 acres of oak wood & parkland. 20 minutes walk from Glendalough, the site of a 6th C. monastic city set in the beautiful "Valley of the 2 Lakes". Very comfortable rooms with lovely views. Open log fires, full-size snooker table, Very quiet & restful. Open all year except Christmas. Children over 12 welcome. Dinner served by 7.30pm, book previous day. 6 en suite rooms.

B25 **FERNDALE**, Josie & Noel Corcoran
ENNISKERRY, CO. WICKLOW.
Tel & **Fax** (01)2863518

B & B £20.00 - £25.00 €24-32
SINGLE SUPPLEMENT £7.00 €9 (only available in off-season).

Victorian house furnished in period style in the centre of Enniskerry village. Beside bus stops & easily accessible from N11. Close to Powerscourt & Wicklow mountains. Dublin 25 mins. Open 1/04 - 31/10. 4 en-suite rooms with tv & tea making facilities.

WICKLOW

B26 **GORMANSTOWN MANOR**, Margaret Murphy
BRITTAS BAY, WICKLOW TOWN
Tel (0404) 69432 **Fax** (0404) 61832 <gormanstown@eircom.net>

B&B £25.00-£35.00 €32-44 **SINGLE SUPPLEMENT** £10.00 €13
DINNER £15.00-£25.00 €19-32

Warmly welcoming, family run, purpose built, farm guest house. Peaceful, stress free atmosphere; quiet spectacular surroundings with landscaped gardens & nature walks. Golf, gardens, heritage attractions, beaches, picturesque mountains, valleys, rivers, lakes, woodlands & breathtaking scenery. Open all year. Credit cards. Children welcome. 10 en suite rooms.

B27 **LISSADELL HOUSE**, Mrs Patricia Klaúe
ASHTOWN LANE, OFF MARLTON ROAD, WICKLOW.
Tel (0404) 67458 <Lissadellhse@eircom.net>

B & B £18.00 - £20.00 €20-22 **SINGLE SUPPLEMENT** £10.00 €13

Perfectly situated on the outskirts of Wicklow town. Part Georgian design, set in own grounds in scenic countryside. 1.5 km from Wicklow, turn right at Grand Hotel (L29A road). AA listed & Karen Brown's recommended. Open 1/03-1/11. Dinner 6.30 pm, book by noon. 25% reduction for children under 10 sharing. 4 rooms, 2 en-suite.

B28 **PLATTENSTOWN HOUSE**, Margaret McDowell
COOLGREANEY ROAD, ARKLOW, CO. WICKLOW.
Tel & **Fax** (0402) 37822.

B & B £21.00 - £26.00 €26 - 33 **DINNER** £16.00 €20
SINGLE SUPPLEMENT £6.00 €8

In 50 acres amidst its own enchanting gardens, overlooking parkland, this charming country residence dating from 1853 is a quiet peaceful haven. On the Coolgreaney Road, 2.5 miles south of Arklow & halfway between Dublin & Rosslare, it is close to sandy beaches, forest walks, golf courses & riding. Warm hospitality awaits you. Credit cards/EC. Open 1/03-01/11, or by arrangement. Dinner 7.30 pm, book by noon. 4 en-suite rooms.

READERS ALSO RECOMMEND in Co. Wicklow

one House, Aughrim, (0402) 36121
B from £40.00 €38. Delightful historic house, superbly restored in remote mountain
ting, an hour from Dublin & 20 min from the sea. 6 en suite rooms

umewood Castle, Kiltegan (0508) 73215 Stunning stately castle B&B £100.00+ €125

athsallagh House, Dunlavin (045) 403112 Golf & swimming in converted stables B&B
0.00++ €76

JBS

elgany Inn, Delgany (01) 2875701 Pub with accommodation B&B about £25.00 €32

he Old Coach House, Vale of Avoca Suzy Caillabet Tel (0402) 35408 Fax (0402)
720 <coach-house@email.com> B&B £25.00 €30. Dinner in the Restaurant £20.00
24 Historic roadside house in the heart of "Ballykissangel" country. 6 en suite rooms

ERITAGE ATTRACTIONS

illrudderry House & Gardens (01) 286 2777 Home of the Earls of Meath built in
e 19th century with the earliest formal garden in Ireland laid out in the 17th century
pen: Apr.-Sept. 1-5p.m. Admission: House & Gardens £4.50 Gardens only £3.00

lount Usher Gardens, Mrs Jay, Ashford, Co Wicklow (0404)40116/40205 10 ha. of
rdant & exotic plants created by 4 generations of the Walpole family along the Dargle
pen Mid March-Oct. Admission £3.50, OAP, Student, £2.50

Thinking of an
Irish holiday?

Renting a
House?

Arranging a Meeting?

Country House Tours

Self Drive or Chauffeur Driven Tours
Itinerary Planning and Reservation Service
Accommodation in Country Houses & Castles
Special Interest Tours
P.O. Box 2281, Dublin 4
cht@tourismresources.ie

Tel: +353 (1) 668 6463   Fax: +353 (1) 668 6578
U.S. Fax: 1 800 688 0363

COUNTY CARLOW

C1 SHERWOOD PARK HOUSE, Patrick & Maureen Owens
KILBRIDE, BALLON, CO. CARLOW.
Tel (0503) 59117 **Fax** (0503) 59355 <info@sherwoodparkhouse.ie>

B & B £27.50-30.00 €25-40 **DINNER** £20.00 €25
SINGLE SUPPLEMENT £7.00 €9

Timeless elegance & warm welcom await you. Georgian farmhouse nestled amid rolling parklands & tranquil countryside. Just off N80 midway Dublin/Rosslare, an accessible country retreat for anyor who enjoys log fires, candlelit dinners, romantic bedrooms with brass & canopy beds. Excellent home cooking. Fishing, riding, pet farm & golfing at Mount Wolseley. Beside Altamont Gardens. Bring your own wine. Small parties catered for. AAQQQQ selected. Credit cards. Open all year. Dinner 8.15pm, book by 3pm. 4 en-suite rooms.

C2 STEP HOUSE, James & Cáit Coady
MAIN STREET, BORRIS, CO CARLOW
Tel (0503) 73209 **Fax** (0503) 73395

B & B from £30.00 €38

A memorable Georgian town house with a neighbouring pub in this picture book village, decorated with impressive antiques which add to the atmosphere for the discerning customer. Open 15/3 - 20/12 Dinner 9.30pm. Credit cards. Wine licence. Unsuitable for children. 5 en suite bedrooms.

READERS ALSO RECOMMEND in Co. Carlow

Kilgraney House, Bagenalstown Tel (0503) 75283 Fax (0503) 75595 Charming & peaceful Georgian rectory with super food & memorable decoration B&B £35.00-£55.00 €44-71 6 ensuite rooms

The Lord Bagenal, Leighlinbridge Tel (0503) 21668 Fax (0503) 21629
<info@lordbagenal.com> B&B £30.00-35.00 Great wine list, good food, on the River Barrow in picturesque village. 12 en suite rooms

whynotireland.com

COUNTY KILKENNY

C3 **ABBEY HOUSE**, Helen Blanchfield
JERPOINT ABBEY, THOMASTOWN, CO. KILKENNY
Tel (056)24166 **Fax** (056) 24192

B & B £20.00 - £30.00 €25 - 38   **DINNER** £20.00 €25
SINGLE SUPPLEMENT £5 €7

Relax in the surroundings of old world elegance in the shadow of Jerpoint Abbey. Ideal location for fishing, hunting, golfing & many scenic routes. AAQQQQ. Mount Juliet Estate 1 mile. Open 31/12 to 23/12. Dinner 7.00pm. Book by 2.00pm. Children welcome. Dogs allowed. Credit cards. 6 en-suite rooms.

C4 **BALLYDUFF HOUSE**, Breda Thomas
THOMASTOWN, CO KILKENNY
Tel (056) 58488

B & B £20.00 - £25.00 €25 - 32   **SINGLE SUPPLEMENT** £5.00 €6

18th C. manor house set in its own grounds, overlooking the River Nore. This charming location is very private; period surrounds ; salmon & trout fishing. Mount Juliet Golf Course & Leisure Centre 5 miles drive; riding, hunting & other activities can be arranged. Film location for 'Circle of Friends' & 'Where the Sun is Rising'. Many beautiful walks on the estate. Children welcome. Open Mar - Oct. 3 rooms, 1 en-suite.

C6 **BLANCHVILLE HOUSE**, Tim & Monica Phelan
DUNBELL, MADDOXTOWN, CO. KILKENNY.
Tel (056) 27197 **Fax** (056) 27636 <blanchvl@indigo.ie>

B & B £30.00-£35.00 €38-44 **DINNER** £22.00 €27
SINGLE SUPPLEMENT £6.00 €7

Elegant Georgian house 10 mins (8Km) from Kilkenny city. Built in 1800 & lovingly restored to give a combination of the atmosphere of a grand era with the comforts of today. Be as active or as relaxed as you wish with golf, fishing, riding, & all the main sporting activities available & a wealth of archaeological & leisure sites to explore. Open 1/03 - 1/11. Dinner 8.00pm, book by noon. Credit cards. Dogs by arrangement.
Children over 10 welcome. 6 en-suite rooms. Enchanting self catering cottage available.

C5 **BERRYHILL**, George & Belinda Dyer
INISTIOGE, CO. KILKENNY.
Tel & **Fax** (056)58434 <berryhil@indigo.ie>

B & B 45.00 €58 **DINNER** £25 €32 by request only
SINGLE SUPPLEMENT £10.00 €13

Charming ancestral home with glorious views of the river & 125 ha. home farm with private Salmon & trout fishing. Wondrous walks, village craft shops & excellent Restaurants. Mt. Juliet Golf Course 5 Miles. 3 Suites, one with verandah. Min. stay 2 nights. Children over 10 welcome open 1 /05-1/11 Wine licence. Credit cards. No dogs please 3 suites with dressing rooms, 1 with verandah.

C7 **CULLINTRA HOUSE**, Patricia Cantlon
THE ROWER, INISTIOGE, CO. KILKENNY.
Tel (051) 423614 (10am-2am) <cullhse@indigo.ie>

B & B £20.00 - £25.00 €25 - 32 **DINNER** £16.00 €20
SINGLE SUPPLEMENT £10.00 €13

Charming farmhouse in 230 acres of woodland at the foot of Mount Brandon with private path leading to Brandon Hill. 6m. from New Ross or Kilkenny road. Cat lovers paradise. Renowned for excellent cuisine, leisurely late night candlelight dinner & breakfasts till mid-day. All booking with Dinner (9.00 - 9.30 pm). Open log fires. Bridgestone Award. Art studio conservatory for guest & conference use. Min. stay 2 nights with dinner. 6 rooms, 3 en-suite

C8 **GARRANAVABBY HOUSE**, Johanna Prendergast
THE ROWER, INISTIOGE, CO. KILKENNY.
Tel (051) 423613

B&B £20.00 €25 **DINNER** £18.00 €23
SINGLE SUPPLEMENT £5.00 €6

Lovely old farmhouse-part late 17th century on outskirts of the Rower village. Scenic setting overlooking a sweep of countryside between Rivers Nore & Barrow. Convenient to Kilkenny Craft Trail & Wexford beaches & golf courses. Animals & poultry always on this working farm. Dinner by candlelight at 7.30pm. Very good cuisine. Excellent restaurants nearby. Rosslare 37 miles. Open Easter - 30/20. 3 rooms.

C9 **SWIFT'S HEATH**, Brigitte Lennon
ENKINSTOWN, CO. KILKENNY
Tel & **Fax** (056) 67653

B & B £30.00 €38 **DINNER** £18.00 €22

Jonathan Swift's boyhood home, this impressive 300 year old house is close to Kilkenny's medieval city, a centre of craft workers. Excellent dinners, using organic farm produce. Grass tennis court, fishing on River Nore, golf & riding nearby, hunting & shooting in season. Dinner by request only, 7.30-8pm, book by noon. Open 1/02 - 20/12. Credit cards. Children over 12 welcome. 3 en suite rooms.

READERS ALSO RECOMMEND in Co. Kilkenny

Bayswell House, Crosspatrick, Johnstown, Carmel Delaney, Tel/Fax (056) 31168 B&B £20.00 €25 Historic farmhouse in remote rural setting. Open 01/05-01/10 3 en suite rooms

Belmore, Jerpoint Church, Thomastown, Rita & Joseph Teesdale (056) 24228 B&B £20-23 €25-29 Fine old family home with gardens & working farm. 3 en suite rooms

Berkeley House, 5 Lower Patrick St, Kilkenny, Declan Curtis & Linda Blanchfield, Tel (056) 64848. Fax (056)64829 B&B £30.00 €38 Central guesthouse in 18th century townhouse Open 29/12-20/12 Credit cards. 10 en suite rooms

Wandersforde House, Castlecomer, (056) 42441 B&B £25.00 €38. Charming and converted School house.

Rathsnagadan House, Inistioge, Pauline Reynolds (051) 423641 B&B £22-£25.00 €30-32 Dinner £21.00 €27. Comfortable & relaxed 19th century farmhouse. Credit cards Open 01/02-01/11 3 en suite rooms

PUBS

The Rising Sun, Mullinvat, (056) 898173 Old world family run inn, 16km from Waterford on the Dublin Road. Good bar food B&B around £20.00 €25

Langtons , 60 John Street, Kilkenny, (056) 65133 A cosy bar leads you into a series of dining rooms. Very smart bedrooms. B&B £50.00+ €63

Kyteler's Inn, Kieran Street, Kilkenny (056) 21064
Booze with a witch in this medieval bar.

Tynan's Bridge House Bar, St John's Bridge, Kilkenny (056) 21291 Superbly preserved Victorian bar - friendly service & a great view of the castle.

CRAFT SHOPS

Nicholas Mosse Irish Country Shop, Bennettsbridge Tel (056) 27505 Fax (056) 27491 Working pottery with a wide selection of other quality crafts

Kilkenny Design Centre, Castle Yard, Kilkenny Tel (056) 22118 Fax (056) 65905 < info@kilkennydesigncentre.iol.ie >A wide range of the best of Irish craft design. Wedding list & mail order available.

HERITAGE ATTRACTIONS

Kilfane Glen & Waterfall, Thomastown (056) 24558 Dramatic scenery & walkways Open May - Sept, Tues - Sun, 14.00-18.00 Adm. £3.00

COUNTY WATERFORD

C10 AGLISH HOUSE, Tom & Terry Moore
AGLISH, CAPPOQUIN, CO WATERFORD
Tel (024) 96191 **Fax** (024) 96482

B & B from £25.00 €32   **DINNER** £20.00 €25
SINGLE SUPPLEMENT £5.00 €6

Between the Knockmealdown Mountains & the sea in the lush Blackwater Valley. Charming old world house with a special ambience. Ideal for a holiday or short break. Peaceful atmosphere, enhanced by fine hospitality & good food. Farmers Weekly recommended. Open all year. Groups catered for at Christmas & New Year. Credit cards. 4 en-suite rooms with TV & telephone.

C11 ANNESTOWN HOUSE, John & Pippa Galloway
ANNESTOWN, CO WATERFORD
Tel (051) 396160 **Fax** (051) 396474 <annestownhouse@eircom.net >

B & B £30.00-35.00 per room €38-44   **DINNER** £20.00 €25
SINGLE SUPPLEMENT £10.00-35.00 €13-44

This utterly relaxing house gazes out to the Atlantic over tennis & croquet lawns. There is space inside & out to spread yourself; the house has been assembled over a couple of centuries so that is rambles over various levels & directions, providing rooms for reading, playing billiards or the piano & ruminating upon the puzzles of love & life. Open 1/3 - 30/11. Dinner 7.00 - 8.00pm, book by noon. Wine licence. Credit Cards. 5 en-suite bedrooms.

C12 THE CASTLE FARM, Emmet & Joan Nugent
MILLSTREET, CAPPAGH, DUNGARVAN, CO WATERFORD
Tel & **Fax** (058) 68049

B & B £25.00 €32   **DINNER** £20.00 €24
SINGLE SUPPLEMENT £10.00 €12

Restored wing of 15th C. castle situated in a picturesque river valley 6km off N72 on R671. Elegantly & comfortably furnished with excellent farm fresh cuisine & a warm welcome. R.A.C. Highly acclaimed. AA QQQQ. Agri-Tourism Award Winner '89 &'95. CIE Tours Awards '89, '90 & '91. Dinner 7pm, book by 12.00. Children welcome; Pets allowed. 01/04 - 01/11. 5 en-suite rooms.

C13 **FOXMOUNT FARM**, David & Margaret Kent
PASSAGE EAST ROAD, OFF DUNMORE ROAD, WATERFORD
Tel (051) 874308 **Fax** (051) 854906 <foxmount@iol.ie>

B & B £30.00 €38   **DINNER** £20.00 €25
SINGLE SUPPLEMENT £7.00 €9

Elegant 17th C. house with log fires, antique furnishings, beautifully decorated in relaxed homely style. AAQQQQ & recommended in many guides for good food & great accommodation. Tennis court. Dinner 7pm, book by 6pm. Do bring your own drink. Open from Mar - Nov. 3 Days D/B/B £145.00. 5 Days D/B/B £230.00. Weekend D/B/B £100.00. Children welcome. 5 en-suite rooms.

C 14 **GORTNADIHA HOUSE**, Eileen Harty,
RING, DUNGARVAN
Tel (058) 46142 **Fax** (058) 46538 <ringcheese@eircom.net>

B&B £25.00 €25-32 **SINGLE SUPPLEMENT** £10.00 €13

Working dairy farm known for its charm and its cheese making. Rural setting close to beaches in Waterford Gaeltacht. Woodland gardens & sea views. Open 01/03 - 15/11 Credit cards 3 en suite rooms

---

C15 **KILMEADEN HOUSE**, Patricia & Jerry Cronin
THE OLD RECTORY, KILMEADEN, CO. WATERFORD.
Tel (051) 384254 **Fax** (051) 384884

B&B £60.00 €76 **SINGLE SUPPLEMENT** £20.00 €25

Elegant Georgian house in 5 ha. of lovely grounds, 10 mins Waterford City on the Cork road (N25). This charming residence has been converted to an exclusive house for discerning guests. Antique furnishings & delightful gardens containing new, rare & well-known plants - a gem. Waterford Crystal 10 minutes. Open -01/05-01/10. Credit cards. Children over 12 welcome. 5 en-suite rooms. Booking essential.

C16 **RICHMOND HOUSE**, The Deevy Family
CAPPOQUIN, CO. WATERFORD
Tel (058) 54278 **Fax** (058) 54988 <richmond@amireland.com>

B & B £45.00 - £70.00 €57-89 **DINNER** £30.00 €37
SINGLE SUPPLEMENT £15.00 €20

Award winning 18th C. country house. Beautifully furnished & decorated, retaining old world charm & character. Ideal for golfing, fishing, sightseeing or relaxing in total tranquillity by log fires. Licensed restaurant with local & French cuisine. Magnificent mountains, woodlands & rivers. Bord Failte 4 star, AA QQQQ, RAC highly acclaimed, RAC Restaurant Award. Open Feb. - Dec. Closed Christmas & New Year. Dinner 7-9pm, book by noon. Credit cards. Full licensed. 9 en-suite rooms.

C17 **SION HILL HOUSE**, Antionette & George Kavanagh
FERRYBANK, WATERFORD CITY
Tel (051) 851558 **Fax** (051) 851678 <sionhill@eircom.net>

B&B £23.00-£30.00 €28-38
SINGLE SUPPLEMENT £4.50-£10.00 €6-12

Charming Georgian manor on 4 acres of park & woodland overlooking the River Suir, an oasis of tranquility beside the city centre. Historic gardens with many rare plants; Antique furnishings. AAQQQQ. Children welcome. Open 8/1-16/12. Credit cards. No smoking house. 4 en suite rooms with t.v. & tea/coffee making facility.

READERS ALSO RECOMMEND in Co. Waterford

Whitfield Court, Waterford (051) 384216 Intriguing architecture, intriguing host, polo school, fairly eccentric B&B around £50.00 €63

PUBS

Bride View Bar, Tallow Bridge, Tallow (058) 56522 Attractive pub overlooking the River Bride. B/B around £15.00 €19

The Moorings Pub, Dungarvan (058) 41461 On the harbours edge in this attractive town B&B about £20.00 €25

Buggy's Glencairn Inn, Glencairn, Lismore (058) 56232 The eccentric Ken Buggy, late of Kinsale, is now the host of this unique & enchanting inn with an excellent dining room.

RESTAURANTS

Dwyer's, 8 Mary St., Waterford Tel (051) 877478 Fax (051) 877480 <dwyerest@eircom.net> Set in an old R.I.C. Barracks Martin Dwyer is a chef of international repute. "Honest, subtle & generous food" The Bridgestone Guide Closed Sun. Dinner from £15.00 €19

McCluskey's Bistro, Paul McCluskey, 18 High St, Waterford (051) 857766 Open Tue.-Sat for lunch & dinner "impressive ingredients, admirably simple cooking" Georgina Campbell's Guide Dinner from £15.00 €19

COUNTY WEXFORD

C18 **CHURCHTOWN HOUSE**, Patricia & Austin Cody
TAGOAT, ROSSLARE, CO. WEXFORD.
Tel (053) 32555 **Fax** (053) 32577 <churchtown.rosslare@indigo.ie>

B & B £25.00-£35.00 €32-45 **DINNER** £21.50 €26
SINGLE SUPPLEMENT £10.00 €13

"A Sense of Tranquillity". Charming period house, originally 1703 elegantly & completely refurbished, in 8.5 acres. AA QQQQQ Premier Selected. Bord Fáilte 4 star. 4 miles from Rosslare ferry port. Traditional country house hospitality, log fires, wine licence, excellent cuisine. Dinner 7.30-8pm. Book by noon. Open 1/03-1/12. Credit cards. Wheelchair friendly. Children welcome. Pets allowed. 12 en-suite rooms.

C 19 **GLENDINE COUNTRY HOUSE**, Tom & Ann Crosbie, ARTHURSTOWN
Tel (051) 389258 **Fax** (051) 389677

B&B £20.00-£25.00 €25-38, **SINGLE SUPPLEMENT** £10.00 €13.

Late Georgian dower house overlooking seaside village. Open 2/01-30/12. Credit cards French Spoken. Children Welcome. Pets Allowed. 5 en suite rooms. Self catering also available

---

C20 **HEALTHFIELD MANOR**. Mayler & Loretto Colloton
KILLURIN, CO WEXFORD.
Tel/Fax (053)28253

B & B £25.00 €32 **SINGLE SUPPLEMENT** £5.00 €6

Georgian Manor House, in beautiful wooded riverside estate. Organically farmed. Near Wexford & Rosslare. Riding, golf & water sports nearby. Open 1/01 - 23/12. Children over 7 welcome. Dogs allowed outside. 3 elegantly furnished spacious bedrooms with romantic panoramic views of the River Slaney. 1 en-suite, 3 with private bathrooms.

C21 HORETOWN HOUSE,
EQUESTRIAN CENTRE & CELLAR RESTAURANT, Ivor Young
FOULKSMILLS, WEXFORD.
Tel (051) 565771 **Fax** (051) 565633 <poloxirl@iol.ie>

B & B £22.75 - £26.75 €28-33 **DINNER** £16.50 - £21.50 €21-27
SINGLE SUPPLEMENT £5.00 €6

300 year old manor house, 23 miles Rosslare Ferry. A farmhouse with a difference. Cellar Restaurant - delicious internationally recommended cuisine. Egon Ronay listed. Equestrian Centre - leisure riding, polocrosse, qualified instructors, all weather indoor arenas, dairy farm. Hydro-Therapy spa. Dinner 6-9pm, book by 4pm. Open all year except Christmas. Weekends - min. stay 2 nights. Dogs by arrangement. Wine licence. 14 rooms, 11 en-suite.

C22 NEWBAY HOUSE, Joan Coyle
WEXFORD, CO WEXFORD
Tel (053) 42779 **Fax** (053) 46318 <newbay@indigo.ie>

B & B from £28.00 €35 **DINNER** £22.00 €28
SINGLE SUPPLEMENT £8.00 €10

Late Georgian residence on 25 acres of gardens & parkland. Wexford 2 miles, close to N11 & N25 & ideal for Rosslare. Near beautiful beaches, archaeological sites, horse riding & golf courses. Renowned for its food & large breakfasts with home-made bread & jam. Period furniture. Dinner served 8pm, book by 6pm. Open all year. Credit cards. 16 en-suite rooms some with 4 poster beds.

C23 SALVILLE HOUSE, Gordon & Jane Parker
ENNISCORTHY, CO WEXFORD.
Tel & **Fax** (054) 35252 <salvillehouse@eircom.net>

B & B £25.00 €32 **DINNER** from £20.00 €25
SINGLE SUPPLEMENT £5.00 €6

Relaxed country house with hillside setting overlooking River Slaney. Recommended by the Irish Food Guide, Bridgestone & Good Hotel Guide. Tennis & badminton lawns; golf nearby. Emphasis on organic produce. Self catering available. Open all year. Dinner 8pm, book previous evening. 5 rooms, 2 en-suite & 1 with private bath.

C24 WOODBROOK, Giles & Alexandra Fitzherbert
KILLANNE, ENNISCORTHY, CO WEXFORD
Tel (054) 55114 **Fax** (054)55671 <ftzhrbrt@iol.ie>

B & B £40.00 - £45.00 €51-58 **SUPPER** £20 €25
SINGLE SUPPLEMENT £10.00 €13

Spacious Georgian house in its own parkland picturesquely set under the Blackstairs Mountains. Spectacular spiral flying staircase & magnificent drawing room. Organic vegetables(Organic Trust symbol) from walled garden. Lovely walks, grass tennis court, good 18 hole golf course 8 miles. Children welcome (no charge if under 10). Credit cards Open June - Sept (& Oct. for Wexford Opera Festival). Dinner 8pm, book by lunch time. Good wine list. 4 large double rooms, 3 en suite, 1 with private bath.

READERS ALSO RECOMMEND in Co. Wexford

Dunbrody House, Arthurstown, (051 389600) a rambling late Georgian house in parkland, it has superb food & delightful accommodation a ferry ride from Waterford & 15 minutes from New Ross B&B around £50.00 €63

Kilmokea House & Gardens, New Ross (051) 388109 Don't miss Mark & Emma Hewlett's wonderful gardens around their 1790s rectory which also offers accommodation from £45.00 €57

Marlfield House, Gorey (055) 21124 Completely over the top & quite self indulgently gorgeous B&B £80.00+ €100

The Old Deanery, Valerie Sinnott Ferns, Co. Wexford (054) 66474 B&B £25.00-£35.00 €32-44. A charming family run Georgian house in the historic town of Ferns exceptional accommodation in a warm & relaxed atmosphere. Open Mar.- Nov. Credit Cards. 4 en suite rooms.

Woodlands House, Philomena O'Sullivan, Killinierin, Gorey
Tel (0402) 37125 Fax (0402) 37133 B&B £25.00-30.00 €32-38 Dinner-£22.50 €29 Georgian house in mature garden setting on river. Open 01/04 - 01/11 Credit cards 6 en suite rooms.

Borrmount Lodge, Guy Urbin, Borrmount, Enniscorthy Tel(054) 47122 Fax (054) 47133 <borrmountlodge@eircom.net> £25.00-29.00 €32-36 Dinner £21.00-£35.00 €27 Purpose built B&B with excellent restaurant beside golf course & river. Open all year. 6 en suite rooms

HERITAGE ATTRACTIONS

National 1798 Visitor Centre, Millpark Rd, Enniscorthy (054) 33540 Multi-media presentation of 1798 Rebellion & good tea-room Mon. - Sat 9.30-6.00, Sun 11.00-6.00 Admission £4.00, Students £2.50

Remember to let your hosts know your arrival time

Be sure to book dinner in advance

Prices are per person sharing based on double occupancy

If you have to cancel there may be a cancellation charge - check when booking

W E X F O R D

COUNTY CORK

D1 **ARDNAGASHEL LODGE**, Jim & Eleanor Ronayne
BANTRY, CO CORK
Tel (027) 51687

B&B £20.00 €25 **SINGLE SUPPLEMENT** £10 €13

Tranquil, private tree lined walks, "Jewel in the forest". Comfortable relaxing modern home, on edge of seaside demesne. Interesting conversations & books. Home baking. Ideal base for touring. Excellent restaurants, pubs, golf & fishing nearby. Safe parking. No smoking. Not suitable for children Open May - Sept. Credit cards. 3 en suite rooms.

D2 **BALLYMAKEIGH HOUSE**, Mrs Margaret Browne
KILLEAGH, CO. CORK
Tel (024) 95184 **Fax** (024)95370 <ballymakeigh@eircom.net>

B & B £35.00 €45 **DINNER** £25.00 €32
SINGLE SUPPLEMENT £10.00 €13

Delightful 18th C. farmhouse in the rich farmlands of East Cork. Housewife of the Year Award, Agritourism Award & Good Hotel Guide Award. National Breakfast Award. AAQQQQ. Superb food, fine wines, leisurely breakfasts. Margaret is a TV chef & cookery writer. Equestrian & Craft centre. Convenient to beaches, Blarney, Fota Park, Ballymaloe & Golf Courses. Children welcome. Open Feb. - Nov.
Dinner 7.30 pm, book by 6pm. Credit cards. Wine licence. 6 en-suite rooms.

D3 **BUTLERSTOWN HOUSE**, Elizabeth Jones & Roger Owen
BUTLERSTOWN, TIMOLEAGUE, BANDON, CO. CORK
Tel & Fax (023) 40137 <mail@butlerstownhouse.com>

B & B £35.00 - £45.00 €44-70 **SINGLE SUPPLEMENT** £5.00

A fine Regency house with magnificent architectural details, in glorious grounds on the Seven Heads peninsula. 1 hr. Cork & 10 mins. historic Timoleague. Ideal for beaches, angling, riding, golf, shooting in season, wooded & coastal walks. Warm hospitality, log fires, 4 poster beds. Open 1/02 - 15/12. Dinner 7.30pm, book by noon. Credit cards. 4 en-suite rooms.

04 CASTLEHYDE HOTEL, Erik & Helen Speekenbrink
ERMOY, CO CORK
el (025) 31865 **Fax** (025) 31485 <cashyde@iol.ie>

B & B from £47.50 €59 **DINNER** from £25.00 €32
INGLE SUPPLEMENT £27.50 €35

Where old met new & became timeless. An 18th C. courtyard renovated to the highest levels of comfort while retaining all its old character & charm. Golf, fishing, hill walking, horse riding locally. Historic sites abound. Mermaids restaurant, the library & lounge with open fires & a heated outdoor pool together with staff dedicated to your comfort & pleasure make for a memorable stay. Open all year. Credit cards. 14 en suite rooms & Self-catering in 5 cottage suites

---

05 CREAGH HOUSE, Michael O'Sullivan & Laura O'Mahony,
DONERAILE, CO CORK
Tel (022) 24433 **Fax** (022) 24715 < creaghhouse@eircom.net >

B&B £55 €70 **SINGLE SUPPLEMENT** £10 €12 **SUPPER** from £10.00 €12

Regency townhouse listed for architecture & history, associated with Thackeray, Sheehan, Bowen, & O'Connell Adjacent to Golf Club & Doneraile Court. Ideal touring base for cultural, historic & sporting sites. Cork, Shannon & Killarney 1 hr. Stately reception rooms, spacious bedrooms & large bathrooms Open Feb. - Nov. Credit Cards 3 en suite rooms

---

06 FORTVIEW HOUSE, Violet Connell
GURTYOWEN, GOLEEN, CO. CORK
Tel/ Fax (028) 35324

B & B £25.00 €32 **SINGLE SUPPLEMENT** £10.00 €13 **DINNER** £19 €25

Traditional stone built house on a diary farm furnished with antique pine. 6 kms from the small fishing village of Schull on the Beara Peninsula. Winner of the National Agri-tourism Award in 1996. AA QQQQ. Extensive breakfast menu.Good restaurants locally. Ideal base for touring West Cork & Mizen Head. Located 2km. from Toormore on main Bantry Road. Dinner 8 p.m., book by 12.00 Open 1/03-1/11 5 en suite rooms.

D7 GLEBE COUNTRY HOUSE, Gill Good-Bracken
BALLINADEE, BANDON, CO. CORK.
Tel (021) 4778294 **Fax** (021) 4778456 < glebehse@indigo.ie >

B & B £22.50 - £35.00 €28-44 **DINNER** £18.50 €23
SINGLE SUPPLEMENT £7.50 - £15.00 €9-19

Charming family run Georgian rectory close to Kinsale & Bandon. Comfortable & relaxed with antiques & coal fires. Take N71 to Innishannon bridge follow signs to Ballanadee. AAQQQQ. Egon Ronay. Dinner 8pm, book by noon Do bring your own drink. Explore quiet country lanes, hidden coves & miles of sandy beaches. Children welcome. Pets allowed. Open 4/01-20/12. Credit cards. 4 en-suite rooms. Self-catering available in old coach-house apartments & chalet Each sleeps 5 & whole for rental, sleeps up to 12.

D8 GLENVIEW HOUSE, Ken & Beth Sherrard
BALLINACLASHA, MIDLETON, CO. CORK.
Tel (021) 631680 **Fax** (021) 634 680 <glenviewhouse@esatclear.ie>

B & B - £40.00 €-51 **DINNER** £20.00 €25
SINGLE SUPPLEMENT £8.00 €10

Georgian home in 10 ha. of mature gardens, surrounded by forestry & woodland walks. In an exceptionally peaceful & scenic area it offers a blend of tranquillity & civilisation, an escape from the bustle of everyday life. Open fires & candlelit dinners.
Midleton 5 km. Ideal for sightseeing, golf & all types of fishing. Enjoy a relaxed country lifestyle, excellent food & a warm welcome. Grass tennis court. Open all year. Dinner 8 pm, book by noon. Wine license Credit cards/Amex. Wheelchair friendly. 4 en-suite rooms. 2 Coach houses- 3 double rooms in each -all ensuite also available.

D9 GROVE HOUSE, Anna & Peter Warburton
SKIBBEREEN, CO. CORK
Tel (028) 22957 **Fax** (028) 22958 <grovhse@indigo.ie>

B & B £27.00-£45.00 €36-57 **DINNER** £16.00
SINGLE SUPPLEMENT £10.00 €13

Restful Georgian home set in 2 acres of gardens & woodland. Open fires, candlelit dinners (book by 12.00), bedrooms with four-poster beds, tv, books, etc. De luxe courtyard suites. Open all year, Credit cards. 8 ensuite rooms. Self-catering in 3 courtyard cottages.

010 **LETTERCOLLUM HOUSE**, Karen Austin & Con McLoughlin
TIMOLEAGUE, CO. CORK.
Tel (023) 46251 **Fax** (023) 46270 <conmc@iol.ie>

B&B £20.00-£30.00 €25-38 **DINNER** £24.00 €31
SINGLE SUPPLEMENT £6.00 €8

A Victorian manor house (c.1860)
beautifully set on 12 acres of
woodland & pasture, overlooking
Courtmacsherry Bay. A place to
unwind, relax, & enjoy the produce
of our organic walled garden & the
best of local meats & seafood. Open
21/3-31/10. Dinner 7.00, book by
Noon. Wine licence. Credit Cards.
Children welcome. 9 en suite rooms.

011 **MARANATHA COUNTRY HOUSE**,
Douglas & Olwen Venn TOWER, BLARNEY, CO. CORK
Tel & **Fax** (021)385102

B & B £19.00 - £25 €24-32 **SINGLE SUPPLEMENT** £6.00 €7

Beautiful private gardens &
woodlands surround this lovely
Victorian country house. Spacious
romantic bedrooms with antiques.
A unique haven of peace surrounded
by majestic shrubs & trees. Ideal for
day trips to Kerry & West Cork, golf,
angling, riding & a selection of
restaurants. Spend a few
memorable days with us. Open
Apr.-Nov. Credit cards. Children
welcome. 5 non smoking en-suite
rooms.

012 **PERRYVILLE HOUSE**, Laura & Andrew Corcoran
KINSALE, CO. CORK
Tel (021) 772731 **Fax** (021) 772298

B & B from £45.00 €57 **SINGLE SUPPLEMENT** £15.00 €19

The perfect balance of luxury,
privacy & location. Poised on the
centre of the medieval fishing port
overlooking the marina this house
combines the grandeur of the past
with the luxuries & convenience of
today. Luxuriously appointed
bedrooms with satellite tv &
telephone. Delicious buffet
breakfast of fresh fruit & cereals,
fresh farmhouse cheeses & home
baked breads & preserves. Open
1/3 - 14/12 & New Year. Credit
Cards. 28 en suite rooms.

D13 **ROCK COTTAGE**, Barbara Klotzer
BARNATONICANE, SCHULL, CO CORK
Tel/Fax (028) 35538

B&B £20.00 - £25.00 €25 - 32 **SINGLE SUPPLEMENT** £10.00 €13
DINNER from £22.00 €28

Georgian hunting lodge on the edge of Dunmanus Bay in 17 acres of wooded parkland, farmland & heather covered hills. Very private, yet close t everything the area has to offer. Dinners (from 7.00, book by noon) are our speciality. Open 1.1-31.12. Credit cards. Children over 10 welcome. 3 en suite rooms.

D14 **SEVEN NORTH MALL**, Angela Hegarty
7 NORTH MALL, CORK CITY.
Tel (021) 397191 **Fax** (021) 300811 <sevennorthmall@eircom.net>

B & B £35. €44
SINGLE SUPPLEMENT £10.00 €13

1750s town house on tree lined mall overlooking River Lee. 4 star elegant accommodation. Superb home cooked breakfast. Adjacent to some of Ireland's best restaurants & pubs. Ideal base for touring city & Southwest. Secure parking. Open from 8/01 -17/12. Suitable for children over 12. Credit cards. 7 en-suite rooms.

D15 **SOVEREIGN HOUSE**, James McKeown
NEWMAN MALL, KINSALE, CO CORK
Tel (021) 772850 **Fax** (021) 774723

B & B £50.00 - £65.00 €63 -80 **SINGLE SUPPLEMENT** £15.00 €19

Former 1708 home to the Sovereign of Kinsale in the heart of the town. Beautifully restored, delightful Queen Ann House, furnished in the Baronial style, with a comfortable atmosphere, lots of exposed stonework, stone flags & all the original fire places & ovens. Sailing & deep sea fishing & 3 superb golf courses, including the remarkable Old Head Course. Open all year except Christmas. Credit Cards. 4 en-suite non- smoking rooms.

D16 **SPANISH POINT SEAFOOD RESTAURANT,**
John & Mary Tattan BALLYCOTTON, CO. CORK
Tel (021) 646177 **Fax** (021) 646179

B & B £25.00 €32 **DINNER** £25.00 €32
SINGLE SUPPLEMENT £5.00 €6

Restaurant & guest house situated on cliff face overlooking Ballycotton Bay. Chef owner, fish caught by own trawler. Golfing, walking, swimming, bird watching, angling, gourmet restaurants. Cork City 45km. Open 14/02- 2/01 Credit cards. 5 en-suite rooms with tv, hair dryers & tea/coffee making.

D17 **TRAVARA LODGE,** Marie & Damien Enright
COURTMACSHERRY, CO. CORK
Tel (023) 46493 **Fax** (023) 46045

B & B £20.00 -£22.00 €22-25
SINGLE SUPPLEMENT
£5.00 €6

Sea facing modernised Georgian terraced house, fishing boats bob a stones throw from the garden. A gaily painted seaside village, sheltered by the woods of the Earl of Shannon's old estate. Lively in summer, exceptional restaurants, beach, pier, angling, riding, bird watching, woodland & coastal walks. Close to Kinsale, Clonakilty, Cork. Open 15/03 to 1/11. Children welcome. Pets allowed. Credit cards. 6 en suite rooms.

D18 **SEA COURT,** David Elder
BUTLERSTOWN, TIMOLEAGUE, BANDON, CO CORK
Tel (023) 40151/40218

B & B from £25.00 €32 **DINNER** £22.50 €29

A fine Georgian house in 5 acres of beautiful parkland on the Seven Heads peninsula. A bird-watcher's & hiker's paradise. Six spacious rooms, many with distant ocean views, all ensuite including the Edwardian Ballroom suite. Open 8/6-20/8. Dinner 7.30pm book previous day. Credit Cards. The house is available for self-catering during the rest of the year.

READERS ALSO RECOMMEND in Co. Cork

Bantry House, Bantry (027) 50047 Historic stately home, stunning setting & gardens, B&B in refurbished wings from £60.00 €76

Barnabrow House, Cloyne Tel/ Fax (021) 652534 B&B from around £30.00 €38. Recently restored 18th C. country house & restaurant next to Ballymaloe. Children welcome 12 en suite rooms.

Bridelands Country House, Crookstown, Macroom (021) 336566 B&B around £30.00 €38

Desmond House, 42 Cork St., Kinsale Tel (021) 4773575 Liam Scally, B&B from £35.00 4 en suite rooms

Farran House, Farran, Patricia Wiese Tel (021)331215 B & B from £45.00 €57 DINNER £25.00 €32 Elegant Country House, in 12 acres of mature beech woods. Large suites, antique furnishings, Open Mar - Nov. 4 en suite rooms.

Flagmount Lodge, Rylan, Nr Macroom, Yvonne Nijs Tel (021) 733 9137 Fax (021) 7339089 <flagmoun@iol.ie> B&B £18.00 €22 Dinner £13.00 €16 Comfortable relaxing & quiet modern house in wild & remote setting Open 1.1-31.12 Credit cards/DC Dutch, French & German spoken. Children welcome. 4 en suite rooms.

Glanworth Mill, Glanworth Tel (025) 38555 Fax (025)38560 < glanworth@iol.ie > B&B from £42.00 €54 Single supplement £10.00 €13. Restored water mill in the shadow of a medieval castle with excellent restaurant Open all year except Christmas. Credit cards 10 double en suite rooms.

Glenally House, Youghal, Tel/Fax (024) 91623 Fred & Herta Rigney, B & B from £35.00 €45 Single supplement £10.00 €13 Dinner £20.00 €26. Late Georgian house on 7 acres of gardens & park, walking distance from town, recently elegantly restored. Open all year, Credit cards, 4 ensuite rooms.

Glenlohane, Kanturk (029) 50014 Anglo-Irish grandeur, American plumbing & retired greyhounds B&B around £50.00 €63

Leighmoneymore Dunderrow Kinsale, Michael & Dominique O'Sullivan Vervaet Tel (021) 4775312 Fax (021) 4775692 < leighmoneymore@eircom.net > B&B 25.00 €30 Large period farmhouse on the banks of the Bandon River. Open 01/03-30/11 Credit cards. 4 rooms, en suite.

The Lighthouse, Kinsale (021) 4772734 B&B from £30.00 €39 eccentric, neo-tudor accommodation 5 en suite rooms.

The Old Parochial House, Castlemartyr, Kathy & Paul Sheehy, Tel (021) 667454 Fax (021) 667429. B&B from £35.00 €44 AA QQQQ Friendly & impressive accommodation in an elegantly restored 18th C. house o n the edge of the village. 4 en suite rooms.

Rathcoursey House, Beth Hallinan, Ballinciurra, Midleton, Tel (021)`613418 <beth@rathcoursey.com> B&B about £45.00 Beautifully decorated very quiet historic house with excellent food 4 en suite rooms.

Seaview House Hotel, Ballylickey, (027) 50073 B&B £45.00-£55.00 €57-70 delightful manor house 17 en suite rooms.

PUBS

The Blue Horizon, Garretstown, Kinsale (021) 4778217 Cosy sea side bar with accommodation. B&B £25.00 €31 4 rooms, 3 en suite.

Mills Inn, Ballyvourney, Macroom Tel (026)45237 Fax (026)45454 B&B about £30.00, food served all day. One of Ireland's oldest Inns (1755) with landscaped gardens 10 en suite rooms

RESTAURANTS

Cork has the reputation of having the best food in Ireland & these are some of the best restaurants in Cork:

Fenn's Quay Restaurant, 5 Fenn's Quay, Sheares St, Cork Eilish O'Leary Tel (021) 279527 Buzzing atmosphere & flavoursome cooking in the heart of the city. Open 10.00 am-10.00 pm Mon. - Sat. Lunch price £8.00 & Dinner £20.00

The Ivory Tower, Exchange Buildings, Princes St, Cork Tel (021) 274665 Continental & multi-ethnic cooking Game & Fish specialties. Evenings only. Average price-£30.00

Jacques Phoenix St, Cork Tel (021) 277387 Fax (021) 270634, Stylish & fun with a new slant on Irish cuisine. Closed Sun. Lunch £10.90 Dinner £21.90

Altar Restaurant, Mike & Peig Ryan Toormore, Goleen (028) 35254 Lunch (£10.00)and Dinner (£25.00) Weds - Sun. B&B £20.00 €25 3 ensuite rooms.

Casino House, Kerrin & Michael Relja Collmain Bay, Kilbrittain, Tel (023) 49944 Fax (023) 49945 A reputation for the best food in west cork & definitely one of the prettiest settings. Open 7 days for lunch (from £14.00) & dinner (£21.00) Self catering cottage available.

The Clean Slate, Midleton (021) 633655 original cooking, worth a detour

Crackpots 3 Cork Street, Kinsale, Co Cork Tel: (021) 4772847 Fax: (021) 4773517 <crackpts@iol.ie> Ceramic Restaurant & Wine bar Excellent original cooking with influences from Japan to Mexico. Pottery workshops for beginners & more experienced or just think about it over a meal or glass of wine. Light Lunch & Dinner £18.00

The Farm Gate, Midleton (021) 632771 & The English Market, Cork, Organic produce amidst contemporary sculpture - great place for a quick lunch.

The Heron's Cove, Sue Hill, The Harbour, Goleen, Tel (028) 35225 Fax (028) 35422 < suehill@eircom.net > B&B £25.00 Lunch £10.00 Dinner £19.50 Seaside restaurant with rooms. 5 en suite rooms.

Restaurant in Blue, Burvill Evans & Christine Crabtree, Schull, Co Cork (028) 28305 Open Wed-Sun, dinner only, from £23.00 a converted stone barn in a wooded cottage garden serving internationally acclaimed natural local food.

CRAFT SHOPS

Boland's, Kinsale Tel/Fax (021) 4772161 A treasure chest of craft-work & clothes collected by Colette Boland. Newsagent, Bureau de change, fax agency & mailing service as well.

The Private Collector, Inishannon (021) 776777 Art ceramics & sculpture.

Keane on Ceramics, Kinsale (021) 4774553 Important sculptural ceramics

COUNTY KERRY

D19 **CARRIG HOUSE**, Frank & Mary Slattery, CARAGH LAKE
Tel (066) 9769100 **Fax** (066) 9769166

B&B from £48.00 €60
SINGLE SUPPLEMENT £25.00 €32

Good food & friendly accommodation in a delightful & somewhat extended historic country house on Caragh Lake with romantic floodlit gardens. Open 3/03-23/12 & New Year. Credit cards 16 en suite rooms

D20 **CASTLEMORRIS HOUSE**, Mary & Paddy Barry
BALLYMULLEN, TRALEE, CO. KERRY
Tel (066) 7180060 **Fax** (066) 7128007

B&B £30.00 €38 **DINNER** £20.00 €25
SINGLE SUPPLEMENT £10.00 €13

Warm welcome awaits you at this Georgian home with private car park & grounds. Relax with complimentary afternoon tea in the drawing room - open fires & friendly atmosphere. Spacious tastefully decorated bedrooms. Home baking & irresistible breakfast menus. Dinner served each evening, book by noon. Wine licence. 8 minute walk from Tralee centre & convenient to Kerry beaches, golf, horse riding, fishing & walking. Open all year. Credit cards. 6 en-suite rooms

KERRY

D21 CLEEVAUN COUNTRY HOUSE, Charlotte & Sean Cluskey.
LADY'S CROSS, MILLTOWN, DINGLE, CO. KERRY
Tel/Fax (066) 9151108 <Cleevaun@iol.ie>

B & B from £19.50 € 24

Galtee Regional Breakfast Winner. In landscaped gardens overlooking Dingle Bay. 2km from Dingle town. Tea/coffee facilities, hairdryers & TV in rooms. Relax & enjoy the magnificent views of Dingle Bay from our breakfast room while you choose from our award winning menu. An oasis of peace & tranquillity. Dinner 7pm. Open Mar - Nov. 9 en-suite rooms

D22 GLENDALOUGH, Josephine Roder-Bradshaw
CARAGH LAKE, KILLORGLIN, CO KERRY.
Tel/Fax (066) 9769156 <deskerry@iol.ie>

B & B £40.00-£45.00 €51-57 **DINNER** £25.00 €32
SINGLE SUPPLEMENT £10.00 €13

Charming and exceptionally comfortable Victorian Country House with magnificent views of Caragh Lake & the McGillycuddy Reeks. Interesting gardens with mature trees & rare shrubs. Woodland walks, hill climbing & golf. A house for all seasons & an excellent base to tour the Ring of Kerry & Dingle's ancient ruins & historic sites. Delicious candlelight dinners 8pm, book by noon. Open 1/03-30/11. Wine licence. Credit cards. Min. stay two nights. 7 Rooms, 6 en suite.

D23 ISKEROON, Geraldine & David Hare
BUNAVALLA, CAHERDANIEL, CO. KERRY
Tel (066) 9475119 **Fax** (066) 9475488 <iskeroon@iol.ie>

B & B £38.00 €46 **SINGLE SUPPLEMENT** £10.00 €13

Overlooking Derrynane Harbour, Iskeroon offers total relaxation & comfort., turf fires, interesting books, a semi-tropical garden leading to a private pier: an ideal base for your stay in Kerry. Open 1/05 to 31/10. 2 night min. stay. Credit cards. Unsuitable for children. 3 rooms with private bathrooms.

D24 **MUXNAW LODGE**, Mrs Hannah Boland
CASTLETOWNBERE RD, KENMARE, CO. KERRY.
Tel (064) 41252

B & B £22.00-24.00 €28-31 **DINNER** £15.00 €19

Wonderful old house built in 1801 overlooking Kenmare Bay. All weather tennis court. Splendid gardens & walks & within walking distance of town. Open all year. Dinner 6.30 pm, book by noon. Dogs allowed outside. 5 en-suite rooms with TV & tea making facilities.

D25 **SALLYPORT HOUSE**, Arthur Family
GLENGARRIFF ROAD, KENMARE, CO. KERRY.
Tel (064) 42066 **Fax** (064) 42067

B & B £40.00 - £45.00 €51-57

Elegant spacious house in peaceful surroundings overlooking Kenmare Harbour. A short walk from the delights of Kenmare including an 18 hole golf course. AA QQQQ. Open 1/04 - 1/11. 5 en-suite bedrooms, TV & direct dial telephone.

D26 **SHELBURNE LODGE**, Tom & Maura Foley
CORK ROAD, KENMARE, CO KERRY.
Tel (064) 41013 **Fax** (064) 42135 <shelburne@kenmare.com>

B & B £35.00 - £50.00 €44-63 **SINGLE SUPPLEMENT** £15.00 €19

Lovely (c1740) Georgian farmhouse in peaceful gardens, 5 mins walk from Kenmare town centre, a gourmet centre with an abundance of good restaurants. Beautiful rooms individually furnished with antiques. Open 1/04 - 31/10. Credit cards. 9 en-suite rooms with direct dial telephone & tv.

D27 TAHILLA COVE COUNTRY HOUSE,
James & Deirdre Waterhouse TAHILLA, NR SNEEM, CO KERRY.
Tel (064) 45204 **Fax** (064) 45104 <tahillacove@eircom.net>

B & B £40.00 €51 **DINNER** £18.00 €22
SINGLE SUPPLEMENT £20.00 €25

Idyllic location on the Ring of Kerry seashore. Owner-run with friendly caring staff. Fully licensed. Tranquility, relaxation & quality home-cooked food, gardens, pier, hill walking, golf, fishing, horse riding locally. Open Easter - mid Oct. Most Credit Cards. Dinner 7.30pm, book by noon. 9 en-suite rooms.

READERS ALSO RECOMMEND in Co. Kerry

Barrow House, West Barrow, Tralee Tel (066) 7136437 Fax (066) 7136402 B&B from £30.0 €38 Historic house by Golf course & sea, now part of The Skellig Hotel Group. 15 rooms ensuite

Beaufort House, Killarney (064) 44764 Pretty 18th C. house & gardens, B&B around £65.0 €70.

Derreensillagh, Tim & Bronwen Youard, Castlecove, Tel (064) 45347 Fax (064) 45588 B&B £30.00 Atlantic views, excellent breakfasts, cottage atmosphere, open all year. 4 en suite room

Gleann Fia, Deerpark, Killarney, Jerry & Nora Galvin, Tel (064) 35035 Fax (064) 35000 <gleanfia@iol.ie> B&B £22.00 - £30.00 €28-38 Single supplement £10.00 €13 Dinner £12.50 €16. Recently built Victorian style country house in 30 acre wooded valley 1 mile from Killarney. Open 1.03 - 1.12 Dinner 6.30 - 7.00, book previous day. Credit cards. French spoken. Children welcome. 17 en suite rooms

The Park Hotel (064 41200) classically traditional & **The Sheen Falls** (064 41600) smooth contemporary - the best hotels in Ireland, rivalled only by each other B&B£100.++ €125

'Rascals' Old School House, Barry's Cross Ballinskelligs Tel/Fax (066) 9479340 < oshmb@iol.ie > B&B £18.00 €22 Dinner £12.50 €15 19th century lovingly restored a mile from sandy beaches Open all year. 7 en suite rooms

Sea Shore Farm, Patricia & Owen O'Sullivan, Tubrid, Kenmare Tel/Fax (064) 41270 < seashore@kenmare.com > B&B £25-£35.00. A charming farmhouse with the amenities of a luxury hotel. Open 1/03-15/11 Credit cards, €31-44 6 rooms ensuite

The Shores Country House, Annette Mahony, Cappatigue, Connor Pass Road, Castlegregory Tel/Fax(066)7139196 < theshores@eircom.net > B&B £19.00-£27.00 €25-35 Single supplement £5.00 €6 Dinner £15.00 €20. Purpose built modern, comfortable designer guest house with sea views. Open 01/02-30/11 Credit cards, 6 en suite rooms

PUBS

The Lake House, Cloonee Tuosist, Kenmare, Mary O'Shea (064) 84205 friendly pub & restaurant in beautiful lakeside setting with guest accommodation. Food highly recommended. B&B under £20.00 €25

RESTAURANTS

Brennans Restaurant, 12 Main St, Cahirciveen, Tel (066) 9472021 Fax (066) 9472914 <brenrest@iol.ie> Lunch at around £10.00 Dinner from £22.00 Local ingredients with seafoo specialties.

CRAFT SHOPS

Louis Mulchahy Pottery, Clogher, Ballyferriter, Dingle, Tel (066) 9156229 Fax (066) 9156366 <clothar@mulcahy-pottery.ie> Ireland's best known stoneware Pottery

COUNTY CLARE

E1 **ARDSOLLUS FARM**, Pat & Loreto Hannon
QUIN, ENNIS, CO CLARE
Tel (065) 6825601 **Fax** (065) 6825959

B & B £19.00 - £25.00 €23-32 **SINGLE SUPPLEMENT** £6.00 €7

A spacious Agri Tourism award winning 300 year old farmhouse on 120 acre working dairy farm overlooking Dromoland Estate. Fifth generation family home There are show jumping horses & ponies on farm. Shannon Airport, Bunratty & Knappogue 15 minutes. 1 mile off N18, turn at Clare Inn. Open 1/04 - 1/11. 4 bedrooms, 2 en suite.

E2 **BERRY LODGE**, Rita Meade
ANNAGH, MILTOWN MALBAY, CO CLARE.
Tel (065) 7087022 **Fax** (065) 7087011 <rita.meade@esatclear.ie>

B & B £20.00-£24.00 €25 -30 **DINNER** - £22.00 €30
SINGLE SUPPLEMENT £10.00 €13

Charming Victorian family home overlooking the sea, a charming blend of old world style & modern comfort. The peaceful atmosphere is enhanced by excellent accommodation & superb food. Hands on cookery classes as part of the holiday available. Ideal for golfing at Lahinch, touring the Burren & Cliffs of Moher. Open 4/02 - 6/01. Special Christmas & New Year break. Dinner 7-9.30pm, book by 2pm. Wine licence. Credit cards. 5 en-suite rooms with tv, tea making facilities.

E3 **HALPIN'S HOTEL**, Pat Halpin
ERIN STREET, KILKEE, CO CLARE.
Tel (065) 9056032   **Fax** (065) 9056317 <halpins@iol.ie>

B & B £27.50-£45.00 €34-51 **DINNER** £20.00 €25
SINGLE SUPPLEMENT £20.00 €19

Highly acclaimed 3 star family run hotel with fine tradition of personal service - a combination of old world charm, fine food, vintage wines, & modern comforts. Views of Victorian Kilkee. Close to Shannon Airport & Killimer/Tarbert car ferry. Ideal base for Kerry & Connemara. Good food, warm atmosphere. Open 15/03-31/10. Dinner 6.30 - 9.30pm. Full licence. Children welcome. Credit cards. 12 en-suite rooms.

E4 **LAHARDAN HOUSE,** The Griffey Family
LAHARDAN, CRUSHEEN, CO. CLARE.
Tel (065) 6827128 **Fax** (065) 6827319

B & B £18.00-£20.00 €23-26 **DINNER** £12.00 €15
SINGLE SUPPLEMENT £5.00 €6

Comfortable home tucked away in a quiet valley on Mid Clare Way with ample room to dine & relax. Fishing, shooting, golf, pitch & putt locally. Trekking holidays arranged. Open Mar - 20 Dec. Credit cards. Dinner 6.30 pm - book by 3 pm. Wine licence. 8 en-suite rooms with direct dial telephone, tv & hairdryer

E5 **LISMACTIGUE,** Michael & Mary Keane
LISMACTIGUE, BALLYVAUGHAN, CO. CLARE.
Tel & **Fax** (065)7077040 <mike-g.keane@analog.com>

B & B £18 €21 **SINGLE SUPPLEMENT** £5.00 €6

Enjoy our hospitality in a 500 year old thatched Cottage. Stay in comfortable but ancient surroundings nestled in the heart of the Burren hills. Ideal base from which to explore this Karst landscape, the Cliffs of Moher, Aillwee Cave & hill walking. Open 1/04-31/9. Fresh spring water supplied to each room. Signposted from the village. 3 en-suite rooms.

E6 **NEWPARK HOUSE,** Mrs Barron & Family
ENNIS, CO CLARE **Tel** (065) 6821233
<newparkhouse.ennis@eircom.net>

B&B £25.00-£30.00 €32-38 **DINNER** £17.50 €23
SINGLE SUPPLEMENT £10.0 €12

An old house of great historic interest, in a woodland setting with large rooms furnished with some antiques. Good food. Convenient to Shannon, Bunratty & the Cliffs of Moher. Turn off the R352 opposite the Roselevan Arms. Open Easter- 30.10 Dinner at 6.30-7.00, book by 3.00. Dogs allowed. 7 en suite rooms.

7 OLD PAROCHIAL HOUSE, Alyson & Sean O'Neill
COORACLARE, KILRUSH, CO. CLARE.
Tel (065) 9059059 **Fax** (065) 9051006 <oldparochialhouse@indigo.ie>

B & B £20-25. €23-30 **SINGLE SUPPLEMENT** £7.00 €9

Escape the pressures & let the world go by in front of turf fires! Victorian priests' residence , now family run furnished with antiques & carefully restored retaining its ornate plaster work, original wooden floors & large bedrooms Set in remote, unspoilt valley with Bronze Age Ringforts, & views across fields to the village, 400m. Ideal base to discover, quiet country roads, friendly locals, spectacular Clare coast (5 minutes drive), Cliffs of Moher & the Burren. Traditional music in pubs. Golf ,fishing; horse riding Children welcome. Credit Cards. Open Apr. - Oct. No smoking. 4 rooms, 2 en-suite with 4 poster bed & 2 with private bathrooms. 3 Self catering apartments in restored stables.

READERS ALSO RECOMMEND in Co. Clare

Carnelly House, Clarecastle, Tel (065) 6828442 Fax (065) 6829222 <rgleeson@iol.ie> Dermott & Rosemarie Gleeson,B&B £87.50 €105 Dinner £30.00 €38, single supplement £37.50 €48. Elegant Georgian splendour, engagingly eccentric hosts, 20 min. from Shannon. Open 15/03 - 15/12. 5 double en suite rooms.

Clifden House, Corofin, Jim & Bernadette Robson Tel(065) 6837692 B & B about £40.00 €44 Idiosyncratic early Georgian house by Lough Inchiquin. Derelict for years, it is being slowly coaxed into compromise with the 21st C. Open all year. 4 en-suite rooms.

Thomond House, Newmarket on Fergus (061) 368304 Smart & elegant neo-Palladian 1960s home of the O'Briens, descendants of Brian Boru B&B around £80.00 €100

Tinarana Health Farm, Killaloe (061) 376966 Sprawling 19th C. house beside Lough Derg B&B £50.00+ €63

PUBS

The Biddy Early, Inagh, Ennis (065) 6836742 Micro brewery & pub, celebrating the last wise woman in Clare!

Cassidy's Bar & Restaurant, Carron (065) 7089109 Country pub off the beaten track in the Burren

Crotty's, Kilrush Tel: (065) 9052470 traditional Irish music, a cosy traditional bar & friendly atmosphere. B&B: around £17.00 €22 Highly recommended

Durty Nelly's, Bunratty, (061) 364072 In the shadow of Bunratty Castle with stone flagged floors & sawdust, a touristy pub patronised by locals.

Linnane's Lobster Bar, New Quay, Burrin, perched on the southern shore of Galway Bay, in the middle of nowhere, rave reviews by food writers

The Cloister's Ennis (065) 6829521 A serious restaurant, good bar food & a chance to drink in holy ground!

The Long Dock Carrigaholt (065) 9058106 Good grub & great craic in a beautiful area

Vaughan's Bar Kilfenora (065) 7088004 Country pub in the Burren, a good place for a snack.

CRAFT SHOPS

Doolin Craft Gallery 065 7074309 Batik & silver from Matt O'Connell & Mary Gray plus a really good craft shop, a fabulous garden & a good food stop

Whitethorn Restaurant & Craft shop Ballyvaughan, Co. Clare (065) 7077044 A In a spectacular setting on Galway Bay. Pleasant self service restaurant, a great craft shop with interesting & well chosen pieces, & an interpretive centre on the Burren & 6 self-catering apartments.

COUNTY LIMERICK

E8 **ASH HILL STUD**, Belinda & Simon Johnson
KILMALLOCK, CO. LIMERICK.
Tel (063) 98035 **Fax** (063) 98752 <ashhill@iol.ie>

B & B £30.00 €38   **DINNER** £20.00-£30.00 €25-38
SINGLE SUPPLEMENT £10.00 €13

A Georgian house of National architectural importance with many fine ceilings & original furnishings. In a well wooded stud farm with riding horses & other farm animals. Home produce used for cooking. Open all year except Christmas & New Year. Dinner from 7pm, book by 10am., 3 en-suite rooms 2 bedroom apartment available .

E9 **BALLYTEIGUE HOUSE**, Richard & Margaret Johnson
ROCKHILL, BRUREE, CO. LIMERICK.
Tel/Fax (063) 90575 <ballyteigue@eircom.net>

B & B - £25.00 €38 **DINNER** £18.00 €22
SINGLE SUPPLEMENT £6.00 €8

Georgian home 2km off N20. Shannon/Cork 1 hr. Good base for touring, riding (horses kept on farm), golf concessions at Charleville, fishing & walking. Warm & happy atmosphere. Bridgestone, AAQQQQQ, Karen Brown & Berlitz. Open 1/03-1/12. Dinner 7 pm, book by noon. Do bring your own wine. Credit cards/AC. 50% discount for children sharing with parents. 5 en-suite rooms. Available to rent on an exclusive basis

E10 **DUNRAVEN ARMS HOTEL**, Bryan F. Murphy
ADARE, CO. LIMERICK.
Tel (061) 396633 **Fax** (061) 396541 <dunraven@iol.ie>

B & B from £62.00 €79   **DINNER** £23.95 + 12.5% S.C. €30

Established in 1792, Grade A 4 star old world hotel situated in the picturesque thatched village of Adar Each bedroom/suite is beautifully appointed with antique furniture. Award winning Restaurant, AA 3 Re Rosettes, Egon Ronay, Gilbey's Gold Medal. Leisure centre comprises 17 pool, gym, steam room & therapy centre. Equestrian, fishing & golfin holidays a speciality. Shannon airport 30 mins. Open all year exce Christmas Day. 76 en suite rooms.

11 REENS HOUSE (On N21), Tilly Curtin
RDAGH, RATHKEALE, CO. LIMERICK
l/Fax (069) 64276 <reenshouse@eircom.net>

& B £25.00 €31 **SINGLE SUPPLEMENT** £7.00 €9

Comfortable 400 year old Jacobean home, on dairy & livestock farm. Situated on Limerick-Killarney N21 road. Adare 10 mins. Shannon 50 mins. A.A.QQQQ, Bridgestone & Elsie Dillard recommended. Ideal touring centre. Golf, fishing & equestrian centre locally. Antique furniture, friendly atmosphere & all modern comforts. Children welcome. Dogs allowed outside.

redit cards. Open 1/04 - 31/10. 4 en-suite rooms.

READERS ALSO RECOMMEND in Co. Limerick

lin Castle, Glin (068) 34112 B&B around £100.00 €125 - The real thing - an Anglo ish ancestral seat, but with plumbing, no spiders & comfort. Also open for tours at rtain times

he Mustard Seed at Echo Lodge, Ballingarry Tel (069) 68508 Fax (069) 68511 B&B 55.00-£80.00 Fab food, brill service, delightful rooms & stunning setting 2 en suite rooms

UBS

innegans, Annacotty, Dublin Road, Limerick (061) 337338 good food & trendy aditional decoration

he Yankee Clipper, Foynes (069) 65700 Pub with accommodation &B about £20.00 €25

oosers Restaurant & Bar Killaloe (061) 376 792 cosy riverside bar & pleasant food.

ERITAGE ATTRACTIONS

oynes Flying Boat Museum, Foynes Tel/Fax (069) 65416 <famm@eircom.net> omprehensive exhibition of a glamorous era in Atlantic air travel, as well as being the ome of Irish Coffee.Open April-October 10 am - 6 pm

COUNTY TIPPERARY

12 ARDMAYLE HOUSE, Annette Vere-Hunt
ASHEL, CO. TIPPERARY.
el (0504) 42399 **Fax** (0504) 42420 < ardmayle@iol.ie >

& B £20.00 €25 **SINGLE SUPPLEMENT** £6.50 €8

Comfortable & spacious farm house, home of the De Vere Hunt family for generations. Situated on 300 acres of farmland where Cattle, horses & sheep graze under old lime & beech trees. Guests are welcome to fish a 2km private stretch of the River Suir. Children welcome. Open 1/04 - 1/10. 5 rooms, 4 en-suite. 2 self catering cottages available.

E13 **ASHLEY PARK HOUSE**, Margaret & PJ Mounsey
NENAGH, CO. TIPPERARY.
Tel (067) 38223 **Fax** (067) 38013 <margaret@ashleypark.com>

B & B £22.00 - £28.00 €25 - 32 **DINNER** £20.00-£23.00 €26-30
SINGLE SUPPLEMENT £5.00 €6

17th c. Country House with private lake for fishing. 70 acres of woodland for those who love tranquil walks & birdwatching. 5 mins from 18 hole golf course. On northern route, centrally located for touring. Watersports, horse riding. Vegetarians catered for. Children welcome. Pets allowed. Open all year. Dinner 8 pm, book by 1 pm. 5 en-suite rooms.

E14 **BALLYOWEN HOUSE**, McCan Family
DUALLA, CASHEL, CO. TIPPERARY.   **Tel** (062) 61265

B & B £25.00 €32 **SINGLE SUPPLEMENT** £7.50 €9 **DINNER** £15 €20

Serene 1750s house listed for its historic & architectural importance. It has been owned by the McCan family since 1864. Set in tranquil surroundings with specimen trees & woodland walks. Open April-Oct. No dogs. Children over 12 welcome. Dinner 7.30, book by 12.00, 4m north of Cashel on N8 road. Take junction signposted Dualla for 1m. 3 rooms, 2 en-suite.

E15 **BANSHA CASTLE**, Teresa & John Russell
BANSHA, CO. TIPPERARY
Tel (062) 54187 **Fax** (062) 54294 < johnrus@iol.ie >

B & B £25 €32 **DINNER** £15 €19 **SINGLE SUPPLEMENT** £6 €7

Beautiful old country house built in 1700's, in lovely wooded grounds & gardens. A warm welcome & superb food make this gracious house your ideal base. Snooker room. Though specialising in relaxation, golf, walking, fishing & horse riding can be arranged locally. Children welcome. Open all year. Special breaks at Christmas & New Year. Dinner 7.30pm, book by noon. Wine licence. 6 rooms, 4 en-suite.

Advance booking recommended. Available for rental.

PUBS

Matt the Thresher Birdhill, Co Tipperary, (061) 379227 A pretty country pub with a view across the Shannon - grab a snack or have a hearty meal

Dwan's Brewery, The Mall, Thurles, Co Tipperary ,Bill Dwan, Tel (0504) 26007 Fax (0504) 26060 < dwan@eircom.net > Micro-brewery in beautiful 19th century granary in the middle of town. Food all day ,live music & beer garden.

Nagles Pub & guesthouse, Kilsheelan, Clonmel, (052) 33496 B&B: £15.00 €19 Family run modern pub on the main Rosslare/Limerick road. 6 rooms en suite.

16 INCH COUNTRY HOUSE & RESTAURANT,
ohn & Nora Egan THURLES, CO. TIPPERARY.
el (0504) 51348/51261 **Fax** (0504) 51754

& B £30.00 €38 **DINNER** £25.00 €33
NGLE SUPPLEMENT £5.00 €6

Historic 300 year old manor on 250 acres. Open fires in dining room & superb William Morris drawing room. Antique bedroom furniture. 16km Rock of Cashel. Ideal for complete holiday or base for touring. Golf, fishing, horse-riding & hunting nearby. Bridgestone best 100. Open 1/01 - 20/12. Restaurant with Cordon Bleu cooking. Dinner 7-9.30pm, book by noon. Credit cards. 5 en-suite oms with tea/coffee facilities, direct dial telephone, TV & hairdryers

17 KILLAGHY CASTLE, Pat & Maria Collins
AULLINAHONE, CO TIPPERARY. **Tel** (052) 53112 **Fax** (052) 53561
killaghycastle@eircom.net>

& B £22.50 - £25.00 €28-32 **DINNER** £18.00 €23
NGLE SUPPLEMENT £10.00 €13

Historic Norman castle sensitively restored with modern comforts. Mature walled garden with lovely mountain views. Perfect for a relaxing or active break. Close to golf courses, angling & walks. Family games room, tennis court. Kilkenny, Waterford, Tipperary, Cork within 40 minutes drive. Highly recommended in travel guides. A genuine welcome combined with real hospitality. Value, comfort & good food await you. . Open 1/02-1/12. Credit cards 5 rooms, 3 en-suite .

18 KNOCKLOFTY COUNTRY HOUSE HOTEL,
tephen Weir & Brona Cullen KNOCKLOFTY,
LONMEL, CO. TIPPERARY
el (052)38222 **Fax** (052) 38300 <knocklofty@eircom.net>

& B £45.00 -£55.00 €57-69 **DINNER** £25 €30 or à la carte
NGLE SUPPLEMENT £50.00 €65

Superbly set in 105 acres of sweeping parkland, over the River Suir, 6km from the Historic Clonmel. A warm welcome, intimate tranquil atmosphere, & people who care about your needs. Once the residence of Lord Donoughmore, the house dates back to the 17th C. Excellent cuisine from inspired chefs. Leisure centre. Tennis court. Horse riding & Golf nearby. 2km private trout & salmon fishing. Children welcome. Pets allowed. Dinner 7-9.30pm, book by 6.00pm. Open all year except Christmas. Full Licence. Credit Cards. 17 en suite rooms.

E19 **KYLENOE**, Virginia Moeran
TERRYGLASS, NENAGH, CO. TIPPERARY.
Tel (067) 22015 **Fax** (067) 22275

B & B £30.00 €38 **DINNER** £23.00 €28

Comfortable 200 year old stone house on 75ha. farm. International horses bred. Clean air, environmentally friendly. Woodlands, birds, deer, red squirrel badgers, rabbits, foxes. High class cuisine, spring water, log fires, warm welcome. Breakfast Award Winner Good Hotel Guide. Adjacent Lough Derg, pubs, good food & music. Golf, riding, sailing, fishing, water skiing, & walks. Children welcome. Pets by arrangement. Wine licence Credit cards. Dinner 8pm, book by 2.30pm. Open all year except Christmas. , 3 en-suite rooms. Stair-lift equipped. Advance booking only.

E20 **MODREENY**, Theresa & Donald Swan
CHARLIE SWAN EQUESTRIAN CENTRE, CLOUGHJORDAN,
CO TIPPERARY **Tel** (0505) 42221 **Fax** (0505) 42128 <cswan@iol.ie>

B&B £30 €38 **DINNER** - Cellar Restaurant **SINGLE SUPPLEMENT** £5. €6

Beautiful historic Georgian family home on 200 acre estate of farm & parkland furnished with family heirlooms. Horse riding, instruction show jumping, country riding, hunting. Swimming pool, garden & games room. Ideal family base for touring. Children welcome. Pets allowed. Golf, tennis, fishing, sailing nearby. Open 2/01 - 20/12. Full licence. Credit cards. 4 rooms.

READERS ALSO RECOMMEND in Co. Tipperary

Annagh Lodge Country House, Coolbawn, Nenagh, Co Tipperary, Rachel & Andrew Sterling Tel/Fax (067) 24225 <annaghlg@hotmail.com>> B&B £25.00 €30 Dinner £20.00. €24 Impressive Georgian mansion with informal family atmosphere on 200 acre farm. Open Apr-Jan, Dinner 8.00, book by 12.00 Credit cards, 4 rooms, 3 en suite

Dancer Cottage, Borrisokane, Tel/Fax (067) 27414 <dcr@eircom.net> Carmen & Wolfga Rodder, B&B £18.00-£20.00 €23-25 Single supplement £3.00 €4 Dinner £16.00 €20 Comfortable modern Tudor Style house in a quiet rural area by an ancient castle highly recommended. Open 1.02 - 30.11. Dinner 7.30, book by noon. Credit cards/Amex. Childre welcome. German & some French spoken, delicious home cooking/baking, 4 en suite room.

Derrynaflan, Ballinure, Cashel, Tel (052) 56406 <dnaflan@iol.ie> Sheila & Edmond O'Sullivan, B&B £20.00 €26, Dinner £13.00 €17, Single supplement £6.00 €7.50 Comfortable 18th Century farmhouse with spacious gardens, excellent food & renowned farmhouse cheese. Open 01/03-01/12. Credit cards, 4 en suite rooms.

Saratoga Lodge, Barnane, Templemore, Tel (0504) 31886 Fax (0504) 31491 Valerie Beamish, B&B £25.00-£30.00 Dinner from £30.00. Elegant Regency dower house attached to stud farm in the Silvermines Mountains, open all year, 3 rooms, 2 en suite.

Somerset, Lorrha, Nr Birr Tel/Fax (0509) 39058 Vera O'Meara, B&B £20.00 €25 Single supplement £5.00 €6 Dinner £18 €22. Open 1.5 - 31.10 Historic house on farm in parkla setting with a Victorian walled garden. Children welcome. Dogs allowed. 4 rooms, 3 en sui

COUNTY GALWAY

F1 CREGG CASTLE, Pat & Anne Marie Broderick
CORRANDULLA, CO. GALWAY.
Tel/Fax (091) 791434 <creggcas@indigo.ie>

B & B £35-45.00 €44-57. **DINNER** £18.00 €22
SINGLE SUPPLEMENT £15.00 €13

A 17th C. castle 15km from Galway city on 80ha. of wild life preserve. Ideal for touring Connemara, Clare, Mayo & Aran Islands. Traditional music around the open fire. Home cooking. Free tea/coffee facilities. Fishing & horse riding nearby. Very friendly atmosphere. Children welcome. Dogs allowed in stables. Open 1/03 -1/11. Dinner 7 pm - book by noon. Wine licence. Groups welcome. Exclusive use by arrangement. Credit cards. 3 family rooms with bath, 5 other rooms, 4 en-suite.

F2 CROCNARAW, Lucy Fretwell
MOYARD, CONNEMARA, CO. GALWAY.
Tel/Fax (095)41068 <lucyfretwell@eircom.net>

B & B from £30.00 €38 **DINNER** £22.00 €28
SINGLE SUPPLEMENT £10.00 €13

A Georgian house on the shores of Ballinakill Bay in lovely prize-winning gardens with an informal relaxing atmosphere, 8km from Clifden. Private fishing. Log fires. Home grown vegetables. Seafood is a speciality in the restaurant. Open 1/05 to 31/10. Christmas & New Year by arrangement. Children welcome. Pets allowed in stables. Dinner 8pm, 24 hours notice required. Full licence. Credit cards. 6 en-suite rooms. Self catering cottage available.

F3 DIAMOND LODGE, Pauline Conroy
KYLEMORE ROAD, LETTERFRACK, CO GALWAY.
Tel (095) 41380 **Fax** (095) 41205 <paulineconroy@eircom.net>>

B & B £20.00 - £27.50 €25-32 **SINGLE SUPPLEMENT** £10.00 €13

A comfortable & cosy hunting lodge, built in 1830, it nestles in woodland under Diamond Mountain, Lovingly restored, furnished in keeping with its period, it houses a unique collection of paintings, & well stocked library for guests to enjoy. Ideal for touring Connemara, Kylemore Abbey, walking in the National Park or local beaches with golf, fishing & horse riding available. Open 1/03-30/10.. Credit cards. Children welcome. Small dogs allowed. 4 en suite rooms.

F4 **KILLEEN HOUSE**, Catherine Doyle
KILLEEN, BUSHYPARK, GALWAY.
Tel (091) 524179 **Fax** (091) 528065 <killeenhouse@ireland.com>

B & B £35.00 - £45.00 €44 -57 **SINGLE SUPPLEMENT** £20.00 €25

Built in 1840 the house is set in 12ha. of grounds down to the shores of Lough Corrib. On the N59 (the main Clifden road) it is an ideal base from which to explore Connemara, The Burren, Aran Islands & Galway. AA QQQQQ. Credit cards. Open all year except Christmas. 5 large en suite bedrooms with antique furniture, telephone, TV, & tea/coffee facility.

F5 **LISDONAGH HOUSE**, John & Finola Cooke
CAHERLISTRANE, NR HEADFORD, GALWAY
Tel (093) 31163 **Fax** (093) 31528 <lisdonag@iol.ie>

B & B £45.00-£60.00 €57-78 **DINNER** £25.00 €32
SINGLE SUPPLEMENT £20.00 €27

A real find! An early Georgian Manor in private woodland overlooking Lough Hackett. Individually decorated bedrooms with "state of the art" bathrooms. Public rooms retain an old world ambience. The cooking is superb, Gourmet Dinner served at 7.30. - book by noon. Wine licence. Children welcome. Dogs allowed outside. Open 01/03-6/12. Credit cards. 10 en suite rooms. Self catering lodge available.

F6 **MOYCULLEN HOUSE**, Philip Casburn
MOYCULLEN, CO. GALWAY.
Tel (091) 555621 **Tel/Fax** (091) 555566 <moyculhs@iol.ie>

B & B £35.00 - £40.00 €44-51 **DINNER** from £23.00 €30
SINGLE SUPPLEMENT £15.00 €19

Cosy 100 year old house in Arts & Crafts Style, surrounded by 33 acres of Rhododendron & Azaleas. 8 miles from Galway city, midway between Connemara & the Burren. Golf, fishing & riding arranged. Superb A la Carte Restaurant, full licence & excellent wine list. Dinner from 7pm. Log & turf fires. Children welcome. Open all year except Christmas &. Credit cards. 3 en-suite rooms.

F7 QUAY HOUSE, Julia & Paddy Foyle
BEACH ROAD, CLIFDEN, CONNEMARA, CO. GALWAY.
Tel (095) 21369 Fax (095) 21608 <thequay@iol.ie>

B & B £35.00-£45.00 €44-57 DINNER £20.00 €25
SINGLE SUPPLEMENT £10.00 €13

Clifden's oldest building, built circa 1820, it has been at various times the harbormaster's house, a monastery, a hotel is now the stylishly decorated home of the Foyle family. Overlooks the harbour with award winning restaurant. All rooms have bath & shower. Children welcome. Pets by arrangement. Dinner 8.00pm. Open Mar - Nov. Wine licence. Credit cards. 14 en-suite rooms.

F8 ROSE COTTAGE, Patricia O'Toole
ROCKFIELD, MOYARD, CO. GALWAY.
Tel/Fax (095) 41082 <conamara@indigo.ie>

B & B £20.00 €25   DINNER £16.00 €20

Family run farmhouse in the Twelve Pins mountain range - the rugged rustic beauty of Connemara. Swimming, fishing, walking, golf, mountain climbing, island trips & much more in the locality. Relax at our open turf fire. Home baking, seafood a speciality. Fruit & herb garden. 4 km Letterfrack & National Park, 8km Kylemore Abbey, 9km. Clifden. Children welcome. National Agri-Tourism Winner, Gault Millau, Karen Brown & many others. Open Mar-Nov. Dinner 7pm book by 4pm. Credit cards. Wine Licence. 8 en-suite rooms with hair dryers & tea making facilities.

F9 ST. CLERAN'S, Elizabeth O'Mahony
CRAUGHWELL, CO. GALWAY.
Tel (091) 846555 Fax (091) 846600 < stclerans@iol.ie >

B & B £85-£130 €215-342 DINNER £34.00 €43
SINGLE SUPPLEMENT £30.00 €38

The film director John Huston's old home has been luxuriously refurbished to 21st century standards & provides stunning yet intimate accommodation in this impressive Regency mansion. Set in 20 ha. of parkland, with woods, trout stream & lake, it is an idyllic haven. Championship golf & riding nearby. Shannon 80 km, Galway 30 km. Open all year. Dinner 7-9 pm, book by 6pm. Credit cards. 12 en-suite bedrooms.

READERS ALSO RECOMMEND in Co. Galway

Castle french, Ballinasloe (0903) 22288 B&B around £65.00 €82. Bill & Sheila Baglaini's stunning 18th. C. mansion, standing in the heart of rolling wooded parkland. Open 01/03-31/10 4 en suite rooms

Cloud 9 Michael & Geraldine Cunningham, Uggool, Moycullen, Tel/ Fax (091) 555390 <cloud9@eircom.net> B&B £20.00 -£28.00 €25 - 35 Single supplement £7.00 €9 A modern home, run with charm & warmth. Open 1.3 - 2.12 Credit cards. 5 en suite rooms.

Delphi Lodge, Leenane, Peter & Jane Mantle, Tel (095)42211 B & B around £50.00 €70 DINNER £30.00 €38 Romantic Georgian country house in remote Connemara Valley. Open 15/01-15/12 12 en-suite rooms.

Kilcolgan Castle, Kilcolgan, Karen Gustafson, (091) 796112 B&B from £70.00 Dinner £25.00-£30.00 Romantic tower on Galway bay. EU 4 rooms. Weekly rental available.

Merriman Inn, Kinvara, Co Galway (091) 638222 Fax (091) 637686 thatched hotel with excellent food & traditional bar. B&B from £35.00 €50 32 en suite rooms

Norman Villa, 86 Lr Salthill, Galway. Dee & Mark Keogh .Tel(091) 521131 B & B about £35.00 Victorian townhouse with brass beds, Irish linen, antique furniture & contemporary art. 5 en-suite rooms

The Angler's Return, Toombeola, Roundstone, Lynnette Hill, Tel (095) 31091 B&B 24.00 €30 Dinner £15-18.00 18th C. fishing lodge. 5 rooms.

Waterfall Lodge, Oughterard , Kathleen Dolly, Tel (091) 552168 B&B £20.00 €25 Single supplement £5.00 €6. AA QQQQ. Pleasant riverside house on outskirts of town. Open all year except Christmas. Children welcome, 6 en suite rooms.

Fermoyle Lodge, Costello, Connemara, Nicola Stronach Tel (091)786111 B & B from £45.00 Wonderful old lakeside lodge, tucked away in a remote part of Connemara with magnificent views, tropical gardens & informal atmosphere. 6 en suite rooms.

Rosleague Manor Hotel, Letterfrack (095) 41101 Fax (095) 41168 B&B £50.00-£75.00 Delightful Georgian country house hotel overlooking the sea, noted for food, hospitality, comfort & views. 20 en suite rooms.

PUBS

Morans of the Weir, Kilcolgan (091) 796113 The most famous thatched oyster bar in Ireland & the only one frequented by Noel Coward & John Wayne!

Paddy Burkes Clarenbridge, Co Galway, Tel (091) 796226 A bustling thatched pub with notable oysters

Busker Brownes, Cross St/Kirwan's Lane, Galway (091) 563377 (bright 'n' breezy seafood bar), Hall of the Tribes (medieval splendour).& The Slate House (cosy coffee house).One venue, three bars, 400 years of history.

E J Kings, The Square, Clifden, Co Galway Tel: (095)-21330/21058 <ejking@eircom.net> Bar food & Restaurant A famous landmark. Traditional Irish music.

RESTAURANTS

Aughrim Schoolhouse Restaurant, Aughrim Co. Galway (0905) 73622, Christopher & Caroline Pele Gourmet cooking around an open turf fire. Average Lunch price £8.00 Average Dinner price £20.00

whynotireland.com

CO. MAYO

F10 CLARE ISLAND LIGHTHOUSE,
Robert & Monica Timmermans
CLARE ISLAND, CO MAYO.
Tel & **Fax** (098) 45120 <clareislandlighthous@eircom.net>

B & B £45.00 €57 **DINNER** £20.00 € 25
SINGLE SUPPLEMENT £10.00 €13

Early 19th C. lighthouse perched on a 387 feet cliff face on Clare Island. Lovingly restored, in keeping with the old world setting. Provides accommodation with unequalled views. Open all year. Dinner 7pm - book by 2pm. Wine Licence 5 en-suite rooms.

F11 DUN MAEVE, Maria Hughes
NEWPORT ROAD, WESTPORT, CO MAYO
Tel (098) 26529 **Fax** (098) 28761 < dunmaeve@anu.ie >

B & B £25-£30 €32-38 **SINGLE SUPPLEMENT** £10 - £30 €13-39

A warm welcome & relaxed atmosphere in the heart of Westport. Victorian town house, renovated with care & attention to detail. Large garden with courtyard & 200 year old coach house. Open 31/12-30/11. Credit cards. 6 en suite rooms

F12 ROSTURK WOODS, Louisa & Alan Stoney
ROSTURK, MULRANNY, WESTPORT, CO. MAYO.
Tel & **Fax** (098)36264 <stoney@iol.ie>

B & B £25.00-£30.00 €32-38
DINNER £25.00 €31
SINGLE SUPPLEMENT £15.00 €19

Good Hotel Guide Cesar Award Comfortable welcoming family home set in secluded mature woodland directly on the sandy seashore of Clew Bay & its islands. Situated between the attractive town of Westport & the renowned landscapes of Achill Island. Antique furnishings, relaxed friendly atmosphere. Hard Tennis Court & Games Room. Golf, riding, sea & lake fishing, boat trips & walking - all nearby. Children welcome. Dogs allowed. Open Feb. -Nov. Dinner 7- 8pm, book 24 hrs in advance. 3 en-suite rooms. Self catering cottage available.

READERS ALSO RECOMMEND in Co. Mayo

Enniscoe House, Ballina, (096 31112) & Belleek Castle, Ballina (096 22400) are romantic historic houses offering varying degrees of eccentricity, fine food & beautiful surroundings B&B from about £40.00 - £80.00 €50-100

PUBS

The Asgard Tavern, The Quay, Westport Tel (098) 25319 Fax (098) 28864 A cosy interior with a good bar menu & a restaurant in the evening

The Riverboat Inn, The Quay, Ballina, Co Mayo, Judd & Jean Ruane, Tel (096) 22183 Fax (096) 72609 Lively pub & seafood restaurant overlooking the Moy.B&B £22.50 €27 8 en-suite rooms.

CO. ROSCOMMON

F13 **GLENCARNE COUNTRY HOUSE**, Agnes Harrington
ARDCARNE, CARRICK-ON-SHANNON, CO ROSCOMMON.
Tel & **Fax** (079) 67013

B & B £22.00 €28 **DINNER** £20.00 €25
SINGLE SUPPLEMENT £5.00 €6

A large Georgian house run by the Harrington family. Log fires & central heating. Home cooking from farm produce. Winner of 3 National Awards. Golf course 1km. N4 route between Carrick-on-Shannon & Boyle. Children welcome. Dinner 7.30pm - book by 6 pm. Wine licence. Open from 1/03 - 15/10. 5 en-suite rooms.

READERS ALSO RECOMMEND in Co. Roscommon

Clonalis House, Castlerea (0907) 20014 Very ugly, quite charming ancestral home of the O'Conors, last high kings B&B around £45.00 €57

PUBS

Bernies Bar, Battlebridge, (078) 20802

The Bridge House Bar, Athleague (0903) 63534 Pub with accommodation B&B about £20.00 €25

Crosby's Pub, Tarmonbarry (043) 26021 Pub with accommodation B&B under £20.00 €25

COUNTY DONEGAL

1 "ARDEEN", Mrs Anne Campbell
RAMELTON, CO. DONEGAL.
Tel/Fax (074) 51243 <ardeenbandb@eircom.net>

B & B £20.00 €25 **SINGLE SUPPLEMENT** £5.00 €6

Old country home overlooking Lough Swilly. Antique furnishings. Private tennis court. Centrally situated for touring Donegal, Glenveigh National Park & Glebe Gallery. Open Easter - Oct. Credit cards. 5 rooms, 4 en-suite. Self catering cottage available.

2 BRUCKLESS HOUSE, Clive & Joan Evans
BRUCKLESS, CO. DONEGAL.
Tel (073) 37071 **Fax** (073) 37070 < bruc@iol.ie >

B & B £25.00 - £30.00 €32-38

An attractive 18th C. house overlooking Bruckless Bay. Irish draught horses & Connemara ponies are bred here. Comfortably furnished with an oriental flavour as the Evans family spent many years in Hong Kong. Fishing, golf & interesting archaeological sites nearby. Open 1/04 - 30/9. Credit cards. 4 rooms, 2 en suite. Self catering lodge available, 2 bed, sleeps 4, from £120.00-£250.00 per week

3 CROAGHROSS, John & Kay Deane
PORTSALON, LETTERKENNY, CO. DONEGAL.
Tel/Fax (074) 59548 < jkdeane@iol.ie >

B & B £20.00 - £30.00 €25-38 **DINNER** £15.00 €19
SINGLE SUPPLEMENT £5.00 €6

A new single storey elegantly furnished country home overlooking Ballymastocker Strand & 18 hole golf course. Fresh seasonal home cooking a speciality. Golfing, swimming, sailing & walking locally. Children welcome. Dogs allowed. New self-catering cottage available. Open 1/04 -30/09. Winter bookings by arrangement. Dinner 7.30 pm - book by 10am. Wine licence. Credit cards. 5 en-suite rooms.

G4 **RHU GORSE**, Gráinne Mc Gettigan
LOUGH ESKE, DONEGAL TOWN.
Tel/Fax (073) 21685 <rhugorse@iol.ie>

B & B £22.50 - £25.00 €25 - 32 **SINGLE SUPPLEMENT** £5.00 €6

Family run country house, surrounded by the Blue Stack mountains & with spectacular view of Lough Eske. Enjoy home baking on arrival & walk in the hills & woodlands of this area of outstanding natural beauty. Children welcome. Open Easter - 31/10. Credit cards. 3 rooms, 2 en suite.

G5 **PORTNASON HOUSE**, Madge & Barry Sharkey
PORTNASON, BALLYSHANNON, CO. DONEGAL.
Tel (072) 52016 **Fax** (072) 31739

B & B £35.00 - £45.00 €44 -57 **DINNER** Groups only
SINGLE SUPPLEMENT £10.00 €13

Seaside Georgian house in 54 acres Private access to sand dune beach. Horse-riding, fishing & birdwatching. A haven for writers, artists & nature lovers. Special interest groups welcome. Open 1/C - 1/10. 10 spacious en-suite rooms.

READERS ALSO RECOMMEND in Co. Donegal

Ardnamona, Lough Eske (073) 22650 Fax (073) 22819 B&B around £45.00 €57
Picturesque lodge, tons of character, lots of charm, stunning gardens, elegant & comfortable reception rooms, 6 excellent bedrooms all with private bath

Castlegrove House, (074) 51118 Letterkenny, Georgian country house hotel B&B fron around £35.00 -£60.00 €44-76 14 en suite rooms

Rathmullan House, Rathmullan (074) 58188 B&B £50.00+ €63
Ignore the chalet scattered parkland & enjoy the view of Lough Swilly

Woodhill House, Ardara (075) 41112 Restaurant with accommodation B&B around £35.00 €44

Frewin, Thomas Coyle & Regina Gibson, Letterkenny Road, Ramelton Tel (074) 51246
< flaxmill@indigo.ie > B&B £30.00-£40.00 €38 -50. Dinner £17.00. Beautiful old rector in 2 acre garden 5 ensuite rooms

PUBS

Leo's Tavern, Meenaleck, Crolly, (075) 48143 Home of Clannad & Enya

McGrorys of Culdaff, Inishowen (077) 79104 Fax (077) 79235 <mcgr@eircom.net>
B&B £30 Musical pub with accommodation

CRAFT SHOPS

The Tannery Design Centre, Drumconnor, Mountcharles, (073) 35675 Julie Griffith knitwear & local pottery, & eclectic contemporary crafts with a café

Open 7 days 10.00-6.00

COUNTY LEITRIM

6 "HOLLYWELL" Rosaleen & Tom Maher
LIBERTY HILL, CARRICK-ON-SHANNON, CO. LEITRIM.
Tel & Fax (078) 21124 <hollywell@esatbiz.com>

B & B £28.00 - £35.00 €35-44
SINGLE SUPPLEMENT £5.00 - £12.50 €6-15

Historic house of great charm in a secluded riverside location. Interesting books. 200 year old tradition of innkeeping. Recommended by major guides. Explore Strokestown Park, King House & Clonalis, Castle Coole, Florencecourt & Marble Arch Caves. Open 1/01- 20/12. Children over 12 welcome. Credit cards. 4 en-suite rooms.

7 GLEBE HOUSE, John & Marion Maloney
BALLINAMORE ROAD, MOHILL, CO LEITRIM.
Tel (078) 31086 **Fax** (078) 31886 <glebe@iol.ie>

B & B £22.00-28.00 €28-35 **DINNER** £15.00 €19
SINGLE SUPPLEMENT £7.00 €9

Lovely Georgian House in woods & farmland. Ideal base from which to explore the North & West. Close to Lough Rynn Gardens, Strokestown House & Marble Arch Caves. Boating can be arranged on Shannon Erne waterways. Open all year except Christmas & New Year. Children welcome. Dogs allowed. Dinner until 9p.m. Wine licence. Credit cards. 8 en-suite rooms.

READERS ALSO RECOMMEND in Co. Leitrim

The Old Rectory, Julie & Patrick Curran , Fenagh, Ballinamore Tel (078) 44089 B&B £18.00-£20.00 €23-26. Georgian home overlooking lake set in 50 acres of wooded parkland. 4 rooms, 2 en suite

Tullaghan House, Tullaghan, Mc Canney Family. Tel (072) 41515/42055 Fax (072) 41515 <emccanney@hotmail.com> B&B £25.00 €32 Single supplement £10.00 €12 Recently restored 18th century manor house between the mountains & the sea, convenient to Sligo, Donegal & Beleek. Open 05/01-23/12 Credit cards, 6 en suite rooms

LEITRIM

COUNTY SLIGO

G8 ARDTARMON HOUSE, Charles & Christa Henry
BALLINFULL, CO SLIGO
Tel/Fax (071) 63156

B&B £25.00-£30.00 €32-38 **SINGLE SUPPLEMENT** £5.00 €6
DINNER £15.00 €19

Family home since 1852, with spacious rooms & period ambience. Secluded grounds, scenic quiet location, & own beach on Sligo Bay. Tennis court. Open 3.1-19.12 Dinner at 7.00, book by noon. Credit cards. 4 en suite rooms. 5 Self catering cottages available, sleeping from 2 - 6, from £80.00-£290.00 per week. 16km NW of Sligo 10 km west of N15 on Drumcliff-Raghly road

G9 MARKREE CASTLE, Charles & Mary Cooper
COLLOONEY, CO. SLIGO.
Tel (071) 67800 **Fax** (071) 67840 <markree@iol.ie>

B & B from £51.50 €66 **DINNER** from £23.00 €29
SINGLE SUPPLEMENT from £8.00 €10

Sligo's oldest inhabited house & home of the Cooper family for 350 years. Magnificent interiors & lovely gardens, combined with a warm welcome & first class food, make Markree Castle a memorable experience. Open all year except Christmas. Riding & instruction available for guests. Dogs allowed. Dinner from 7.30. Full licence. Credit cards. 30 en-suite rooms.

G10 MARKREE HOUSE, Anthony & Lydia Murray
COLLOONEY, CO. SLIGO.
Tel (071) 67466 **Fax** (071) 69667 <markree@eircom.net>

B & B £25 €30

Large & attractive country house, superbly set on 62 acres. Bordered by the River Unshin & adjacent to Markree Castle. Delightful accommodation. Seclusion & tranquility assure you a memorable stay. Dogs allowed in stables. Open 1/04 - 31/10. Strictly no smoking. 3 en-suite rooms.

11 **TEMPLE HOUSE,** Sandy & Deb Perceval
ALLYMOTE, CO. SLIGO.
(071) 83329 **Fax** (071) 83808 <guest@templehouse.ie>

& B from £42 €53-59 **DINNER** £19.00 €23
NGLE SUPPLEMENT £10.00 €6

A Georgian mansion in 500 ha. of farm & woodlands, overlooking a 13th c. castle. The Percevals' home since 1665, refurbished in 1864, it retains its old atmosphere with open fires & some canopied beds. Dinner 7.30 pm - book by noon. - using produce from the estate. Terraced gardens, woodland walks, bird watching, boats (pike fishing),

arby golf, riding, trout lakes, archaeology, mountains, beaches. We often accompany
ests to traditional music sessions & dances. Wine Licence. Open 1/04 - 30/10. Credit
rds. 5 en-suite rooms. Sandy has allergies so no perfumes or after shaves please.

READERS ALSO RECOMMEND in Co. Sligo

oopershill, Riverstown If Markree & Temple are full & you want a elegant hospitality
u will find it within this Bindonesque cut stone elegance
71) 65108 B&B £50.00+ €63

JBS

rgadons, O'Connell St., Sligo Tel: (071) 70933 A legendary pub with a wonderful
spoilt interior.

COUNTY ANTRIM

H1 **THE BEECHES COUNTRY HOUSE**, Mrs Marigold Allen
10 DUNADRY ROAD, DUNADRY, CO. ANTRIM BT41 2RR.
Tel/Fax (028) 9443 3161 **Fax** (028) 9443 2227 <reception@thebeeches.org

B & B £30.00 **DINNER** from £15.50 **SINGLE SUPPLEMENT** £5.00

On the A6 at Dunadry, this seclude Edwardian residence in mature landscaped grounds offers quiet rural accommodation with a friendly atmosphere. Noted for excellent breakfast & home made soups. Airport 3 miles, Larne Ferri (Antrim Coast) 17 miles, Belfast 12 miles. Golf/fishing nearby. Open Feb. - Dec. Taste of Ulster award fo past 7 years. No smoking. Credit cards. 5 en-suite rooms with TV, tea/coffee, trouser press, etc.

H2 **CRAIG PARK**, Jan & David Cheal
24 CARNBORE ROAD, BUSHMILLS, CO ANTRIM BT57 8YF
Tel (028) 20732496 **Fax** (028) 20732479 < jan@craigpark.co.uk >

B & B from £25.00 SINGLE SUPPLEMENT from £5.00

Comfortable Country House 2 mil from Bushmills & close to the Gian Causeway. Good beaches nearby. Dramatic scenery. Fantastic walks, cycling & golf. We prefer guests n to smoke. Children welcome. Ope 1/01 - 20/12. Credit cards. 3 en-suite rooms with tv & tea/coffee making.

READERS ALSO RECOMMEND in Co. Antrim

Drumadoon, Pearl Mitchell, 236 Frocess Road, Cloughmills, BT44 9PX (028) 276 3873 B&B from £27.50 Avant garde rococo decoration in a charming 18th century home 5 en suite rooms.

Maddybenny Farm House, Loguestown Rd., Portrush, (028) 708 23394 B&B from about £25.00 3 en suite rooms

PUBS

Matties Meeting House 120 Brustin Brae Road, Cairncastle, Ballygally 028 2858 32

The Thatch Inn 57 Main St Broughshane (028) 2568 6727

The Bushmills Inn, Bushmills (028) 2073 2339 Old coaching inn with 30 rooms B& about £50.00

Fullerton Arms, Anne & Lyle Taggart, 22 Main St Ballintoy Tel/ Fax (028) 207 69613 Pub with accommodation meals all day. Music Thurs - Sun. B&B £25.00 11 en suite rooms

The House of McDonnell, Tom O'Neill, 71 Castle St., Ballycastle Tel (028) 2076 29 A traditional pub that has remained virtually unchanged since 1744. Traditional music weekends.

Prices in Northern Ireland are in Sterling £.

OUNTY DOWN

BEECH HILL, Victoria Brann
BALLYMONEY ROAD, CRAIGANTLET, HOLYWOOD,
DOWN BT23 4TG
& **Fax** (028) 90425892 <Beech.Hill@btinternet.com>

B £30.00 **SINGLE SUPPLEMENT** £5.00

This stunning home is situated in farm land of the peaceful Holywood hills, 15 minutes from The Belfast Ferries, Belfast City Airport, Bangor, Newtownards & 10 excellent golf courses. A wonderful friendly home brimming with style. The en suite bedrooms are beautifully decorated with antiques, have direct dial telephone, TV, tea/coffee making facilities etc. AA premier select QQQ. Credit cards. Private parking. Open all year. Dogs allowed in kennels. Children 12 welcome. 3 ground floor en-suite double rooms.

CARRIG-GORM, Elizabeth & Roland Eves
BRIDGE ROAD, HELEN'S BAY, BANGOR,
DOWN BT19 1TS
(028) 9185 3680

B from £25.00 **SINGLE SUPPLEMENT** from £5.00

A part Victorian & part 18th C. house set in secluded gardens. Six golf courses within 5 miles. Folk & transport museum & good restaurants nearby. Log fires in lounge hall. Children welcome. Open all year except Christmas & New Year. 3 rooms, 1 en-suite.

EDENVALE HOUSE, Gordon & Diane Whyte
PORTAFERRY ROAD, NEWTOWNARDS, BT22 2AH
DOWN. **Tel** (02891) 814881 **Fax** (02891) 826192

B £27.50 **SINGLE SUPPLEMENT** £5.00

Beautifully restored Georgian house in a delightfully secluded parkland & gardens with private parking. 20 Min. Belfast City Airport`. Beside Mount Stewart House & the National Trust Wildfowl Refuge. Extensive views of the Mournes over Strangford Lough. Windsurfing, birdwatching & golf nearby. AA 5 Diamonds. Open all year except Christmas. Children welcome. Dogs allowed in kennels. Credit cards 3 en-suite rooms.

**To call Northern Ireland from outside the UK prefix
the number listed with +44 & drop the initial 0.**

D
O
W
N

H6 SYLVAN HILL HOUSE, Jimmy & Elise Coburn
76 KILNTOWN ROAD, DROMORE, BT25 1HS, CO. DOWN.
Tel & **Fax** (028) 9269 2321

B & B £25.00   **DINNER** £15.00   **SINGLE SUPPLEMENT** £5.00

Listed Georgian "one & a half storey" house set in mature trees, mountain views, within easy reach of National Trust Properties, Ards Peninsula & Antrim coast. Log fires, delicious food, 30 mins from both airports, near Hillsborough. 2 miles from Dublin/Belfast road. Dinner 8.00pm book by 10am. Open all year. 3 rooms, 2 en-suite

READERS ALSO RECOMMEND in Co. Down

Tyrella House, Downpatrick David & Sally Corbett, (028) 4485 1422 Informal Georgian house in great seaside setting B&B around £40.00

The Narrows, Portaferry Will & James Brown, Tel (028) 4272 8148 B&B from around £ 40.00 Very modern guest house in 18th C. quayside buildings. 13 en suite rooms

Barnageeha, Ardmillan, Killinchy, BT23 6QN Denis Crawford, Tel (028) 541011 B&B £25.00 Dinner from £20.00 Excellent food in modern house overlooking Strangford Lough. Open all year 3 en suite rooms

PUBS

Chestnut Inn 28 Lower Square, Castlewellan,(028) 4377 8247 Pub with accommodation B&B around £25.00

Denvirs, English St., Downpatrick (028) 4461 2012 Historic Inn with excellent home cooking & accommodation B&B around £25.00

Dufferin Arms Coaching Inn, 35 High Street, Killyleagh, Co Down BT30 9QE Tel:(028) 4482 8229 Fax:(028) 4482 8755 <dufferin@dial.pipex.com> In the shadows of Killyleagh Castle & on the shores of Strangford Lough, great evening food, music on Saturdays, accommodation & atmosphere. B&B £32.50 Credit cards 7 en suite rooms

Portaferry Hotel Waterside village inn (028) 4272 8231 B&B from £40.00

Slieve Croob Inn, 119 Clanraghan Rd, Castlewellan (028) 4377 1162 Pub with accommodation B&B around £25.00

The Hillside 21 Main Street, Hillsborough, Co Down Tel (028)9268 2765 Pleasant pub in elegant town

RESTAURANTS

The Anchorage Restaurant 49 Main St, Groomsport, Co Down: Tel:(028) 9146 5757 Fax:(028) 9147 9863 Modern cooking, a modern restaurant & an ancient building. Lunch: £18.00 Dinner: £22.00.

Remember to let your hosts know your arrival time

Be sure to book dinner in advance

Prices are per person sharing based on double occupancy

If you have to cancel there may be a cancellation charge - check when booking

OUNTY FERMANAGH

ARDESS HOUSE & CRAFT CENTRE, Brian & Dorothy Pendry
SH, CO FERMANAGH, BT93 1NX.
(028) 6863 1267   <ardess@clara.net>

B £22.50   **DINNER** £12.50   **SINGLE SUPPLEMENT** £5.00

Ardess (1780) is in secluded woodland with gardens, peacocks & Jacob sheep. Imaginative cooking including vegetarian using produce from organic kitchen garden. Guests may join in the Craft Centre activities including spinning, weaving & painting. Open 15/01-15/12. Dinner 8 pm - book by noon. Dogs allowed outside. Credit cards. 4 en-suite rooms.

READERS ALSO RECOMMEND in Co. Fermanagh

ssfad House Mrs LA Williams, Killadeas, Ballinmallard, BT94 2L3 Tel (028)
88505 B&B £20.00 Single supplement £5.00 Enchanting 18th century house with
ghtful gardens, 5 miles from Enniskillen. 2 en suite rooms

npo Manor, Tempo Enniskillen BT943PA John and Sarah Langham 028 6654 1450
from £65. Ancestral home oozing history. 4 en-suite rooms.

BS

e Lanesborough Arms High St., Newtownbutler (028) 67738488

ohan's Fiddle Stone, 15-17 Main Street, Belleek, Co Fermanagh Tel: 013656-
08 Traditional Pub in the centre of Belleek, home of the famous pottery, on the banks
e River Erne. B/B around £20.00

OUNTY LONDONDERRY

STREEVE HILL, Peter & June Welsh
DOWLAND ROAD, LIMAVADY,
. LONDONDERRY BT49 0HP.
(028) 77766563

B from £45.00   **DINNER** £30.00   **SINGLE SUPPLEMENT** £10.00

A most attractive & very comfortable house, fine gardens & mature woodland. Really superb cooking. An ideal place for self indulgent relaxation. Dinner 7.30-8.30pm - book by 10am. Open all year. 3 en suite rooms.

READERS ALSO RECOMMEND in Co. Londonderry

Ardtara Country House Hotel, 8 Gortleade Rd., Upperlands, BT46 5SA Tel (028) 79644490 Fax (028) 79645080. Victorian manor house, large luxuriously furnished rooms with antiques. 8 en suite rooms. B&B from £50.00

Camus House, Josephine King, 27 Curragh Road, Castleroe, Coleraine, BT51 3RY Tel (028) 7034 2982 B&B about £25.00 attractive 18th century farmhouse. 3 rooms, 1 en suite.

Drumcovitt House, Florence & Frank Sloan, 704 Feeny Road, Feeny BT47 4SU Tel (028) 7778 1224 B&B from £22.00 If you can do without en suite bathrooms, this is a very special, beautiful & memorable place to stay.

Greenhill House, Aghadowey, Coleraine, Tel (028) 7086 8241 B&B from around £25.00

The Old Rectory, Joan & Peter Pyne, 16 Queen St., Derry BT48 EQ Tel (01504 269691 B&B £25.00. City centre Georgian townhouse in conversation area. Well & comfortably furnished & decorated. 6 rooms, 1 en suite.

The Faerie Thorn Bar Main St Tobermore (028) 7964 4385

COUNTY TYRONE

H9 **GRANGE LODGE**, Ralph & Norah Brown
7 GRANGE ROAD, MOY, DUNGANNON, BT71 7EJ,
CO. TYRONE.
Tel (028) 8778421 **Fax** (028) 87723891

B & B £34.50   **DINNER** from £22.00   **SINGLE SUPPLEMENT** £14.50

This exquisite Georgian retreat offe comfort, true family hospitality & graciously appetising dining. With 10 mins drive there is a variety of attractions - Tyrone Crystal, The Argory (National Trust), the ances home of US. President Grant & Armagh - the ecclesiastical capital Ireland. Golf, swimming, squash, boating coarse & game angling & riding nearby. Dinner 7.30pm bool by noon. Open 01/02 - 20/12. Children over 12 welcome. Dogs outside only. 5 en-suite rooms.

READERS ALSO RECOMMEND in Co. Tyrone

McGirrs, The Square, Coalisland, (028)8774 7559 Pub with accommodation

HERITAGE ATTRACTIONS
Ulster American Folk Park Omagh, Co Tyrone Tel: 01662 256 Fax 01662 242421 <uafp@iol.ie> The Emigration story told in vivid form. Open: April-September all week 11.00-6.30 Oct.-Mar Mon. - Fri. 10.30 - 5.00 Entrance: £4.00, Students £2.50

CRAFT SHOPS
Suitor Gallery, Ballygawley Roundabout, Co Tyrone (028) 85568653 Wide variety of crafts & unusual gifts & tea shop Open Tues-Sat 10.00-5.30 & Bank Holidays.

Havens & Hideaways

Offer over 100 manor houses, castles and
cottages of character for weekly rental.
Many of our homes are featured at
www.tourismresources.ie/cht

Prices range from £250.00 a week for a traditional 2
bedroomed mountain cottage to £25,000.00 a week for a
12 bedroomed luxury castle with full staff.

A few of our properties:- Kinsale: A
historic manor house, it is furnished
with solid 18th century furniture
including 4 poster beds. Though the
setting is very remote it is only 20
minutes from the Old Head Golf
Course. It can sleep up to 10 people in
4 double rooms. £2,500.00 per week.

Killarney: One of the finest
Georgian homes in Kerry, the
beautifully converted stable yards
which are surrounded by wooded
parkland, paddocks and gardens,
provide accommodation for up to
people in 11 twin or double
bedrooms, all with private bath. There is a pub within
walking distance! £2,400.00 per week.

Wexford: Wrapped around a 16th
century castle this riverside home
offers accommodation for up to
12 guests within 90 minutes of
Dublin £3,000.00 per week.

Midlands: Traditional mountain
cottage with 2 bedrooms, simply
furnished with country pine.
£250.00 per week.

Limerick: Romantic castle with 7 bedrooms, sauna,
billiards room, tennis court, at the heart of hundreds of
acres of woodland, and farm. £2,000.00 per week

Havens & Hideaways
PO Box 2281 Dublin 4, Ireland
t: +353 1 668 6463 f: +353 1 668 6578 e: cht@indigo.ie